Captain John Smith
Revised Edition

Twayne's United States Authors Series

Pattie Cowell, Editor

Colorado State University

TUSAS 177

CAPTAIN JOHN SMITH

Captain John Smith's portrait is from the map of New England in Smith's A Description of New England *(1616).*

Captain John Smith
Revised Edition

Everett Emerson

University of North Carolina at Chapel Hill

Twayne Publishers • New York
Maxwell Macmillan Canada • Toronto
Maxwell Macmillan International • New York Oxford Singapore Sydney

Captain John Smith, Revised Edition
Everett Emerson

Twayne Publishers   Maxwell Macmillan Canada Inc.
Macmillan Publishing Company   1200 Eglinton Avenue East
866 Third Avenue   Suite 200
New York, New York 10022   Don Mills, Ontario M3C 3N1

Library of Congress Cataloging-in-Publication Data

Emerson, Everett H., 1925–
    Captain John Smith / Everett Emerson. —Rev. ed.
       p.   cm. —(Twayne's United States authors series)
    Includes bibliographical references and index.
    ISBN 0-8057-3989-0
    1. Smith, John, 1580–1631. I. Title. II. Series.
F229.S7E44   1993
973.2′1′092—dc20   92-29055
                                   CIP

10 9 8 7 6 5 4 3 2 1

Printed in the United States of America.

This book
is dedicated to the memory of
Philip L. Barbour

Contents

Preface

Captain John Smith saved the youthful Virginia colony; named New England; visited the Balkans, Turkey, Russia, southern, central, and western Europe, the Caribbean, and the American coast as far north as modern Maine; and wrote enough about America and his adventures to fill three fat volumes.

From his own time at least until 1953, when Bradford Smith's biography appeared, Smith was usually seen as a liar and a braggart. It was easy to dismiss even his considerable accomplishments as the one person responsible for the survival of the first permanent English colony in the New World, that of Jamestown, because Smith lacked modesty in his account of what he had done. It was even possible to think that his reputation would have been greater had he never chosen to write at all. Now, 400 years after his birth, Captain John Smith has at last arrived.

Anyone who is attracted to Captain John Smith, either the man of action or the writer, must be gratified by the recent history of his reputation. Thanks largely to the heroic scholarly labors of the late Philip L. Barbour, who was both Smith's biographer and his editor, Captain John Smith is recognized as a highly important figure in both early American history and early American literature. I am grateful to Mr. Barbour, who received me at his Newtown, Connecticut, house that he called *The Arn*—because it had been a barn but had suffered a partial loss. I saw him there after he had finished his splendid biography but before he had begun his magisterial complete edition. His two volumes published by the Hakluyt Society—*The Jamestown Voyages Under the First Charter, 1606–1609* (1969)—had been completed, but not yet published. At *The Arn* I saw a scholar at work in a huge study, big enough for a separate area for each of his four current projects. He had on hand the mammoth Soviet encyclopedia as well as books in many languages, and not just the more familiar ones. Mr. Barbour shared information with me in conversation and correspondence, and in turn, to my great satisfaction, he frequently cited my 1971 study in his edition. Mr. Barbour died on 21 December 1980, his eighty-second birthday. Fortunately his edition of *The Complete Works of Captain John Smith* was sufficiently advanced—the editorial work was completed—that it could be published, after necessary delays, in 1986.[1]

The Barbour edition is one of the great achievements of modern scholarship. As a longtime specialist in early American literature, I see it as a major landmark. With this new edition, and other important research of the last 20 years, contributions available to me, I was delighted to have the opportunity to rewrite my own literary study of Smith. My work was also assisted by the publication in 1991 of *Captain John Smith: A Reference Guide*, prepared by Kevin J. Hayes, which provides access to scholarship that appears to have escaped even the diligent efforts of Mr. Barbour.

The publication of the Barbour edition was the occasion of a grand stocktaking and reassessment of Captain John Smith's importance. One historian reached the following judgment: "Smith is valuable because he gives us the means of watching the transformation of North America, in English perceptions, from an undesirable obstacle to a land of opportunity and a home for a transatlantic European population. Smith, in a sense, was present at the creation, and it is through his work that we, too, can witness the Big Bang."[2]

One of the reasons that Smith has assumed a position of importance is that he is the first American writer writing in English and is now regularly identified as such in anthologies of American literature.[3] But a question has naturally arisen—can one call Smith an American writer? He was in America less than three years. In his essay "Captain John Smith: American (?)," J. A. Leo Lemay ably argues that we may call him an American—and an important personage—for four "literary and intellectual reasons": "1, Of any known early colonists, Smith had the grandest—and the most radical—secular vision of the meaning of America. 2, Smith was the best promotion writer during the crucial period of American colonization, 1607–1631. 3, Smith first tried to define what it meant to be an American and first claimed that American identity was distinctive and desirable. And 4, Smith thoroughly identified with America."[4] Few would deny that Captain John Smith played a vital role in the early history of America, including a formulation of what America was to be.

Since I wrote the first edition of this work, my own appreciation of Smith has grown, in part because of the appreciation expressed by others. Taking part in the celebration of the publication of the Barbour edition in Williamsburg, Virginia, was especially important to me: though I admired Smith before, I am now even more an enthusiast. But I have left the contours of my study what they were in 1971. Chapter 1 seeks to supply a context for an understanding of Smith's works. The literary background of Smith's historical writings, reports, and propaganda is not well-known; moreover, many of the works that I take up were used by Smith in preparing his own works, especially his *Generall Historie*, which is largely a compilation of others' writings. Chapter 2 provides information on Smith himself needed to understand his writings, nearly all of which are in a sense autobiographical. Chapters 3–8 examine and analyze the works themselves and look at such matters as Smith's originality, the forces that shape what he wrote and the relationship of the works to the author's principles and ideals. Finally, chapter 9 offers an appraisal of Smith's accomplishment as writer. Because I want to make Smith's writings—and those of other writers of the sixteenth and seventeenth centuries—as accessible as possible, I have modernized spelling, capitalization, the use of italics, and paragraphing.

The reader of Smith's works has the pleasure of hearing his voice and of knowing as well what the man looked like. In *A Description of New England* Smith provided in the upper left-hand corner of a map of New England a half-length portrait of himself, with full, rounded beard and mustache (see frontispiece). Smith's left hand holds the hilt of his sword; his right is on his hip. His eyes look out, unabashedly. One may well be reminded of the portrait of Walt Whitman that introduces the first edition of *Leaves of Grass*. In both instances, we are intended to remember the author's appearance as we read.

Acknowledgments

Quotations from Charles Olson's *Maximus Poems*—edited by George Buttrick; copyright © 1983 The Regents of the University of California—appear with the kind permission of the University of California Press. I am grateful to Michele Ware and most especially my wife Katherine for careful reviews of my manuscript.

Chronology

1605–1606   Returns to England. Works with Bartholomew Gosnold in making plans for the Virginia colony.

1606   Departs in December for America with more than 100 colonists on three ships.

1607   Arrives in March in the West Indies; in late April at Chesapeake Bay. Appointed to governing council of seven but is not for a time permitted to serve, perhaps because of insubordination. Settlement established at Jamestown; Smith takes notes about events. In September, appointed supply officer. Captured by the Indians.

1608   Taken to Powhatan, leader of Virginia Indians, and rescued from death, according to Smith's account, by Pocahontas, Powhatan's daughter. Made Powhatan's son and named Nantaquas. In May, sends to England an account of happenings in Virginia, which is published later in the year as *A True Relation*. Explores Chesapeake Bay and the Potomac River. Elected president by the governing council.

1609   Badly burned in a powder explosion; returns to England in October.

1610–1611   Works on material published in *A Map of Virginia*.

1612   Publication of *A Map of Virginia*.

1614   Sails for America in March; arrives in Maine in late April. Explores Maine and Massachusetts coast. Returns to England in August, with plans for a colony in the area he names New England. Appointed Admiral of New England by Plymouth Company.

1615   Sails for America in the spring. When his ship is unable to continue, returns to England and sets out in a smaller ship. Soon captured by pirates, who take Smith on board. Escapes to France; finally returns to England where he writes *A Description of New England.*

1616   Publication of *A Description of New England*. Visits Pocahontas, who is married to John Rolfe, in London. Plans new venture to America.

1617   Prepares to sail with three ships to New England. Delayed by winds for three months; expedition canceled.

1618	Requests a financial grant from Lord Francis Bacon to start a colony in New England.
1618–1619	Seeks means to return to America.
1620	Publishes *New Englands Trials*.
1622	Enlarged edition published of *New Englands Trials*.
1622	Requests the Virginia Company to send him to Virginia to avenge a massacre.
1623	Publishes prospectus of *Generall Historie*.
1624	Publication of *Generall Historie*.
1626	Publication of *An Accidence*.
1627	Publication of an enlarged edition of *An Accidence*, entitled *A Sea Grammar*.
1629	Prepares *The True Travels*.
1630	Publication of *The True Travels*.
1631	Publication of *Advertisements For the unexperienced Planters of New England*. John Smith dies on June 21.

Chapter One
The America of the Elizabethans

Captain John Smith as adventurer and writer stood in the tradition of the great Elizabethan voyagers. Like them, he sought to extend English power; and, like some of them, he provided posterity with reports of his adventures; for, as he wrote in his autobiography, "Many of the most eminent warriors and others, what their swords did, their pens writ" (III, 142). John Smith's life and works are what Irving Story has called them, "a climax to an English sequence extending over half a century."[1] Through Smith, America came to share in the tradition of the Elizabethan voyagers, and an understanding of Smith requires some familiarity with them.

The end of the Elizabethan Age and the early years of the seventeenth century were for England an age of foreign travel, for men's horizons had widened with the discovery of the New World. For England, what has been called the Age of Drake began as early as 1562, when John Hawkins transported a cargo of slaves from Africa to the West Indies to trade to the Spaniards for sugar, hides, and pearls. Of no great significance in itself, the voyage had important consequences. It offered encouragement to the English to do additional business in the Caribbean, though the Spanish authorities did not welcome Englishmen in what they considered their exclusive territory. When a later voyage by Hawkins led to disaster—the Spaniards nearly destroyed a fleet of six English ships in the West Indies—Francis Drake, who had served with Hawkins, sought to outwit the Spaniards and avenge the loss by raiding the Isthmus of Panama in 1572. Drake seized a rich hoard of precious metals near Nombre de Díos; then, in 1577–80, while circumnavigating the globe, he raided Spanish ports and ships on the coast of Peru.[2]

These events created great excitement in England, for they revealed the riches available in the New World. Earlier, in 1493, Pope Alexander had established the principle that lands discovered not belonging to a Christian prince were the property of the prince under whom the discoveries were made. John and Sebastian Cabot's explorations of 1497–98 had given England claim to at least a part of the North American coast.[3] England, however, had been too poor to try colonization at that time. By the 1580s, England could no longer resist the temptation to establish its own colonies.

A Colony in Newfoundland

The one part of America well-known to Englishmen was the coast of Newfoundland, where the fish caught on the nearby banks were salted, dried, and shipped home. These processes took place only in the late spring and summer, and the winter weather was unknown. If a colony were to be established in Newfoundland, it was thought, fishing might be more profitable: salt could be made there, and drying apparatus could be kept ready for use. The English believed that food was readily available, as well as iron, copper, and timber.

The patent for colonization of the area was held from 1578 to 1584 by Sir Humphrey Gilbert; and, though he was more interested at first in piracy than in colonies, he planned a settlement. After mustering funds, he sailed in June 1583 for Newfoundland with five ships and 260 men. The largest ship, supplied by Sir Walter Raleigh, soon deserted, but the remaining voyagers crossed the seas and established themselves. In their efforts to extend their claim, they ran into bad weather, one ship hit a shoal, and nearly all the intended colonists drowned. Gilbert headed back to England, still determined to try again in the spring. But near the Azores the remaining ships hit rough water, and Gilbert and his ship went down.[4] Despite this disaster, a very favorable—indeed, eloquent—report of the expedition was prepared by Edward Hayes, captain of a surviving ship, who was optimistic about the commodities of Newfoundland:

We could not observe the hundredth part of creatures in those uninhabited lands, but these mentioned [Hayes's catalogue occupies two pages] may induce us to glorify the magnificent God, who hath superabundantly replenished the earth with creatures serving for the use of man, though man hath not used a fifth part of the same, which the more doth aggravate the fault and foolish sloth in many of our nation, choosing rather to live indirectly, and very miserably to live and die within this realm pestered with inhabitants, than to adventure, as becometh men, to obtain an habitation in those remote lands in which nature very prodigally doth minister unto men's endeavors, and for art to work upon.[5]

Richard Hakluyt

Hayes's account was published by Richard Hakluyt (1552–1616), a clergyman. English interest in colonization is intimately connected with his work. At Oxford University, where he had been a student during the years 1577–82, Hakluyt read whatever he could locate in modern and ancient languages concerning discoveries and voyages. Then as lecturer on cosmology at Oxford, he found himself seeking out sea captains and merchants for more information. He corresponded with the Flemish geographer Gerhardus Mercator, probably the leading geographer of all Europe. In 1580, Hakluyt began the work for which he was to become famous: he published two narratives by Jacques Cartier on the discovery of the Saint Lawrence River. (Hakluyt had the translation made by John Florio, later the noted translator of Montaigne.) The preface expressed the hope that the work might induce Englishmen to establish a colony in America. Much more important was Hakluyt's publication in 1582 of *Divers Voyages touching the discovery of America.* In it he attempted to establish, through reports of the Cabot discoveries, the English title to North America. He also collected French and Italian documents that supplied information about America, and he prepared an extended list of American commodities and a discussion of the Northwest Passage.[6]

Later Hakluyt composed two other influential works. The first was *A Particular Discourse of Western Planting* (1584). Intended to induce Elizabeth to plant colonies in America, it set forth a colonial policy based on economic needs, provided an augmented list of the supposed riches of America, and offered a program for colonization.[7] If its influence on Queen Elizabeth was slight, it had its effect; it was read by men such as Sir Walter Raleigh.[8] It is the most important statement of the case for English colonization. But Hakluyt's greatest work came a few years later. *The Principall Navigations, Voiages and Discoveries of the English Nation* (1589; revised and enlarged, 1598–1600) fills 11 volumes in a modern edition. Hakluyt's documents report on far more than travel to America: they treat the Near and Middle East, Africa, and Russia. They include reprints from older books, reports written at Hakluyt's request, materials from his own notes, translations, and captured foreign documents. The influence of Hakluyt is perhaps best suggested by Michael Drayton's ode "To the Virginian Voyage," written in 1606, just before the Jamestown colonists set out. The ode begins:

> You have heroic minds
> Worthy your country's name,
> That honor still pursue
> Go, and subdue,
> Whilst loit'ring hinds
> Lurk here at home, with shame.

It ends:

> Thy voyages attend,
> Industrous Hakluyt,
> Whose reading shall inflame
> Men to seek fame,
> And much commend
> To after times thy wit.

Of Hakluyt's work, A. L. Rowse has written ". . . the focusing of the nation's interest upon America . . . was largely due to the life's work of the younger Hakluyt: it has been given to few men to fertilize the history of their country so prodigiously."[9] Hakluyt also gave England preeminence in making accounts of voyages and travels available in print.

Motives for Colonization

English motives for colonization were many. Louis B. Wright cites five: (1) the desire to convert the Indians to Protestant Christianity (the Spanish effort to convert the Indians to Catholicism was considered highly undesirable); (2) the expectation of riches, such as the English had captured from the Spanish colonies; (3) the need to establish new markets; (4) the attraction of exotic fruits, herbs, gums, drugs, and other raw materials; and (5) the patriotic desire for an English empire.[10] Specifically, the English were attracted to North America—or Virginia, as they then called the whole area north of Florida—because they might find the Northwest Passage to Cathay, because of the Cabot voyages, because the temperate zone would supply a market for woolens, and because the Spaniards and Portuguese had effectively sealed off Central and South America.[11] The fact that they were mostly interested in the North did not preclude the English from expecting miracles of the sort that the Spaniards had found in the South. As Eva G. R. Taylor states, "overseas lands spelt minds of gold and silver, markets where silks and spices could be purchased for a song, or failing these, such lands were dismissed as savage and hideous wastes, not worth a moment's consideration."[12]

English efforts to discover a Northwest Passage, though futile, played a role in the story of English colonization overseas; for English exploration in the Northwest, especially that of Martin Frobisher, convinced "the English that their seamen were equal to the hardest test that the world could offer, and yielded some part of that immeasurable confidence that the ocean was their field of fame."[13] Colonies were naturally associated with this conviction. The defeat of the Spanish Armada in 1588 increased English self-confidence.

The Roanoke Colony

After Gilbert's 1583 effort, Sir Walter Raleigh attempted in the 1580s to establish a permanent colony at Roanoke in what is now North Carolina. Karen Kupperman notes, "Colonies such as Roanoke were placed farther south than they should have been in order to be a better base for privateering."[14] The Roanoke colony, now famous as the Lost Colony, was described in a work that did something to satisfy the developing English appetite for accounts of the strange new worlds to the west.[15] The book is especially valuable, and its author, Thomas Hariot (sometimes Harriott), is an important precursor of Captain John Smith.

Thomas Hariot graduated from Oxford University in 1580. A few years later, during the winter of 1583–84, he was employed by Sir Walter Raleigh to teach him cosmology and navigation, presumably as preparation for a project that Raleigh had in mind, for it was in the spring of 1584 that Raleigh sent two ships to explore the American coast. They visited the chain of North Carolina islands just offshore known as the Outer Banks, and brought back to England two Native Americans, Manteo and Wanchese. Possibly Hariot was on one of these ships; in any case, either from his experience in America or from the two Native Americans Hariot learned enough of the Algonquian language to permit him to communicate when he journeyed to the North Carolina coast the next year as scientific observer. Another important member of the team was John White, an excellent watercolorist, whose pictures vividly render the flora, fauna, and inhabitants of the area explored. The English ships arrived on the American coast in late June of 1585, and in September the explorers established a colony on Roanoke Island. Hariot explored the wide area from Ocracoke Island to modern Norfolk, Virginia. In America for almost a year, he learned a great deal about the place and its people. In proper scientific fashion, Hariot kept a journal, which he was later required by Raleigh to turn into a systematic history of both the 1584 and 1585–86 ventures. Neither the history nor the journal was published, and neither, unfortunately, is extant. The only surviving record of his investigations is a work written to promote the area. Although composed in the winter of 1586–87, *A brief and true report of the new found land of Virginia* was not to appear until 1588, when it was published to show that Sir Walter Raleigh was still vitally interested in the so-called Virginia ventures.[16] Then in 1590 it was published in Latin, French, German, and English with engravings based on the marvelous watercolors that John White had made from his observations. David B. Quinn calls the volume "the most delectable of Americana."[17] Addressed thus to an international audience, it became a famous book.

In Hariot's account, America is presented not as a place where one might make a home but as a source of riches that could be exported to Europe. Hariot reduced the strange new world to the ordinary. He provided the first description of tobacco in English, but instead of describing the lift that smoking provides, he presents it as a tonic: by its means the Indians "are notably preserved in health and know not many grievous diseases wherewithal we in England are oftentimes afflicted." Hariot's description of the New World is organized into categories: first, merchantable commodities; then "such commodities as Virginia is known to yield for victual and sustenance of man's life"; then "commodities for building and other necessary uses." Only after all of these catalogues does he finally describe "the natures and manners of the people."[18]

Hariot's descriptions are graceful, scientific, and of practical application. "Cedar, a very sweet wood, and fine timber, whereof if nests of chests be there made of timber thereof, fitted for sweet and fine bedsteads, tables, desks, lutes, virginals, & many things else. . . ." The sweet wood becomes fine timber and then quickly "sweet and fine bedsteads" (9). Fortunately, many readers of Hariot's account read it in the international edition prepared by Theodore de Bry, with the invaluable illustrations derived from White's drawings that are described on the title page of the second part of the volume as "the True Pictures and Fashions of the People in that Parte of America now called Virginia." As Wayne Franklin has noted, "The Virginia scene as rendered by de Bry became . . . a . . . nearly romantic locale. . . ."[19] De Bry's engravings provide pictures of a conjurer, a group of Indians praying with rattles about a fire, a dance with "every man attired in the most strange fashion they can devise" (64), the tomb of the Indian chiefs, and many portrayals of the daily lives of the Native Americans and their flora and fauna.

The most valuable part of Hariot's report concerns the Indians. Here he was less concerned to propagandize than to demonstrate that he had been successful at learning a great deal about the peoples that the English intended to intrude upon. De Bry's volume with Hariot's text had 17 printings in the next 25 years and was considered "the leading, the most scientific, authority, for the best part of a century."[20] Because Hariot's account is often compared with John Smith's portion of *A Map of Virginia*, it is well to note the differing circumstances of the composition of the two: Smith prepared his book—without benefit of notes—several years after his Virginia adventures, whereas Hariot wrote soon after his voyage from an extensive record of observations made *in situ*.

Hariot was convinced that North Carolina was an excellent site for a permanent colony. He liked the climate and the fertility of the soil, and he admired Sir Walter Raleigh's generosity: Raleigh would grant "five hundred acres to a man only for the adventure of his person" (32) He saw no difficulties that would prevent the establishment of a prosperous colony. The Indians, he reported, "are not to be feared, but they shall have cause both to fear and love us that shall inhabit with them" (24).

Though unrealistic in their optimism, Hariot's comments about the Indians are generally well informed. He seems to have developed a good acquaintance with their language. Frequently he provides Indian names for what he describes, and he may have prepared a dictionary of Indian words. Quite possibly he shared some of his knowledge with Captain John Smith, who showed in Virginia a good deal of insight into Indian language and behavior. Hariot's discovery that the Indians were fascinated with scientific and mechanical devices, such as guns and burning glasses, may also have been useful to Smith. The Indians seem to have viewed these devices in much the same light as the Bible, intro-duced without much effect by the earnest missionary Hariot. All were regarded as miraculous.[21] *A brief and true report* is so attractive and valuable that it is a pity the chronicle of the expedition mentioned by Hariot is not extant. An account prepared by the governor of the Roanoke Colony, Ralph Lane, and published by Hakluyt in 1589, is much less significant than Hariot's work.[22]

Raleigh and Guiana

The Roanoke colony's failure resulted from the fact that war with Spain in 1588 intervened and from a lack of long-range planning and substantial investment. Raleigh was interested in quick returns, and Spain was almost an obsession with him. He was determined that England should not be second to her dreaded enemy; and, because he believed the key to Spain's power to be the gold that her South American colonies provided, he wanted to obtain comparable wealth for England. He therefore began to collect information about Spanish explorations in South America; he soon began to focus on Guiana. Hakluyt had observed in 1582 in his *Discourse of Western Planting* that Europeans had not yet taken over Guiana, which it was thought might be the location of the famous "El Dorado."

Students of American literature know of "El Dorado" as the legendary land sought by Edgar Allan Poe's gallant knight, but the legend has a basis in history. At the sacred lake of Guatavita in the uplands of Bogotá, the Indian chief performed a solemn religious ceremony of sacrifice each year until the Indians lost their independence. First the chief anointed his body with oil; then he rubbed it over with gold dust. In this gilded appearance he travelled to the center of the lake by canoe, sacrificed offerings of gold and other precious objects to the lake, and finally jumped into the water and bathed. The story of the gilded man (*el hombre dorado* or *el dorado*) and his rich empire spread, but its exact location was lost.[23]

Raleigh believed that Guiana was "a country that hath yet her maidenhead, never sacked, turned, nor wrought . . ." (73). English ships had frequently visited Trinidad, which was an appropriate base for operations; therefore, Guiana seemed accessible, and in 1594 Raleigh had needed a solution to his problems. He had lost his standing with Queen Elizabeth in 1592 when he had married Elizabeth Throckmorton, a maid of honor at court. He had even been imprisoned for a time, and his finances were not what he wanted them to be. To redeem himself, he later wrote,

I did therefore even in the winter of my life [he was about 40, but men lived shorter lives in those days] undertake these travels, fitter for boys less blasted with misfortune, for men of greater ability, and for minds of better encouragement, that thereby, if it were possible, I might recover but the moderation of excess and the least taste of the greatest plenty formerly possessed. If I had known other way to win, if I had imagined how greater adventures might have regained, if I could conceive what farther means I might yet use, but even to appease so powerful displeasure, I would not doubt but for one year more to hold fast my soul in my teeth, till it were performed. (3–4)

So Raleigh went to Guiana. He was away from England less than eight months; and when he returned, some even doubted that he had made the trip. To remove these doubts and to persuade the Queen to invest in other adventures in Guiana, Raleigh wrote *The Discoverie of the large and bewtiful Empire of Guiana*, which was so popular that it required four editions in 1596. (It was later reprinted by Hakluyt.) Though Raleigh, in fact, had discovered nothing, the area having been explored earlier by the Spaniards, his book is one of the masterpieces of Elizabethan travel writing.

While Raleigh's aim throughout the work was propaganda, he clearly had persuaded himself that the area was capable of supplying England with immense wealth. The country, he reported,

hath more abundance of gold than any part of Peru, and as many or more great cities than ever Peru had when it flourished most. It is governed by the same laws, and the emperor and people observe the same religion and the same form and policies in government as was used in Peru, not differing in any part, and as I have been assured by such of the Spaniards as have seen Manoa, the imperial city of Guiana, which the Spaniards call el Dorado, that for the greatness, for the riches, and for the excellent seat, it far exceedeth any of the world, at least of so much of the world as is known to the Spanish nation. It is founded upon a lake of salt water of 200 leagues long, like unto *mare caspium*. (17)

In *The Discoverie of . . . Guiana*, Raleigh prefaced his own story with an extended history of Spanish activities in the Orinoco River area. Despite his tough-mindedness and skepticism, Raleigh accepted the existence of Amazons "not far from Guiana," whose queens each April met with kings of adjacent countries for sexual intercourse. The daughters so conceived were retained by the Amazons, while the sons were handed on to their fathers (26–27). With similar credulousness he told of being given for food an armadillo, "all barred over with small plates somewhat like to a renocero, with a white horn growing in his hinder parts, as big as a great hunting horn, which they use instead of a trumpet. Monardus[24] writeth that a little of the powder of that horn put into the ear cureth deafness" (50–51).

Raleigh and his men first established a base on the southwest corner of Trinidad. After having the good fortune to capture Fernando de Berrio, the chief Spanish explorer of Guiana, they prepared vessels for the trip up the Orinoco. They then crossed to the mainland, a distance about the width of the English Channel, travelled through the delta, then reached the savannah country, and finally, the main stream of the Orinoco. Raleigh found the country astonishingly attractive: "we passed the most beautiful country that ever mine eyes beheld, and whereas all that we had seen before was nothing but woods, prickles, bushes, and thorns, here we beheld plains of twenty miles in length, the grass short and green, and in divers parts groves of trees by themselves, as if they had been by all the art and labor in the world so made of purpose. And still as we rowed, the deer came down feeding by the water's side as if they had been used to a keeper's call" (42). C. S. Lewis calls the description "enchanting," and Raleigh's work as a whole he finds possesses "almost every charm that a prose narrative could."[25]

The English were careful to treat the Indians with special care, Raleigh reported, for they hoped to make them allies against the Spaniards, whose treatment of the Indians was infamous. Raleigh wrote with pride of the care given Indian women by the men of his company. The passage is unusual because the sexual relations of English and Indians are seldom discussed in the travel literature of this period. Raleigh protested "before the majesty of the living God that I neither know nor believe that any of our company one or other, by violence or otherwise, ever knew any of their women, and yet we saw many hundreds and had many in our power, and of those very young and excellently favored, which came among us without deceit, stark naked" (44).

As they sought to continue inland, the explorers were blocked by a great escarpment. One way to reach the plateau beyond seemed to be by means of the Caroni River, but the heavy summer rains had increased the size and vigor of the stream so that it was impossible to go on. Besides, they could see in the distance 10 or 12 waterfalls, "every one as high over the other as a church tower" (54).

Raleigh's evidence for the area's wealth certainly seems inadequate, and he brought back little of value. He did not have equipment to obtain samples, though he writes that he and his men saw "all the hills with stones of the color of gold and silver" (63). Nevertheless, he could promise that "The common soldier shall here fight for gold and pay himself instead of pence with plates half a foot broad, whereas he breaketh his bones in other wars for provan [food] and penury. Those commanders and chieftains that shoot at honor and abundance shall find there more rich and beautiful cities, more temples adorned with golden images, more sepulchres filled with treasure than either Cortez found in Mexico or Pizzaro in Peru" (71). Raleigh himself had seen none of these riches.

To demonstrate his intention to return to the area, Raleigh left behind a boy and a man, but lack of any real indications that wealth was available made it impossible for Raleigh to go back. If his book did not have the result he sought, it did much to increase Englishmen's interest in the worlds beyond the horizon and thus prepared the way for other colonies. It should be added that Raleigh finally returned to Trinidad in 1618 in a last attempt to reestablish himself with Guianan wealth, but the results were catastrophic. Raleigh's son was killed and his trusted colleague Laurence Keymis, unable to find the mine that he had been telling Raleigh about for 23 years, committed suicide in despair. Raleigh's supply of ideas was exhausted. All that remained was the splendid dream that he was able to capture only on paper.

A Visit to Cape Cod

The next significant effort at colonization took place in the spring and early summer of 1602 and was a project inspired by Richard Hakluyt and undertaken by Bartholomew Gosnold, who served as captain on the voyage, and Gabriel Archer, who intended to establish a trading post in the New World. (Gosnold probably was to recruit Captain John Smith for the Jamestown expedition, and Archer was to be a fellow colonist). In the same year as their voyage, 1602, an account of it, entitled *A Brief and True Relation of the Discoverie of the North part of Virginia* and written by the Reverend John Brereton, was published. The author had probably served as chaplain on the expedition.[26] Brereton's attractive pamphlet is too little known, although a condensed version was published by Captain John Smith in the first book of *The Generall Historie of Virginia, New-England, and the Summer Isles*, and another was prepared by William Strachey for his *Historie of Travell into Virginia Britannia*.

The 1602 expedition, the first by Englishmen to the shores of New England, was expected to serve as a prelude to colonization. The company first saw land at the rocky coast of what is now southern Maine, where they were met by a group of Indians, some of whom seem to have traded with Spanish fishermen. At any rate, "one of them [was] apparelled with a waistcoat and breeches of black serge, made after our sea-fashion, hose and shoes on his feet" (145). Because of uncertain weather and "no very good harbor," the English decided to head southward. After half a day's sail in a stiff breeze they reached a "mighty headland," which they found to be a peninsula. There the fishing was excellent, with codfish in abundance. (Not noted in Brereton's account was the fact that Captain Gosnold decided to name the peninsula Cape Cod after the fish they found there.) Sailing round the tip of the cape, they came to several attractive islands. Brereton and some others went ashore on one, which they named Martha's Vineyard for Gosnold's daughter. Brereton's description of the island is almost ecstatic:

The chiefest trees of this island are beeches and cedars, the outward parts all overgrown with low, bushy trees, three or four feet in height, which bear some kind of fruit, as appeared by their blossoms: strawberries, red and white, as sweet and much bigger than ours in England, raspberries, gooseberries, hurtleberries [huckleberries?], and such an incredible store of vines, as well in the woody part of the island, where they run upon every tree, as on the outwards parts, that we could not go for treading upon them; also many springs of excellent sweet water, and a great standing lake of fresh water, near the sea side, an English mile in compass, which is maintained with the springs running exceedingly pleasantly through the woody grounds which are very rocky. Here are also in this island great store of deer, which we saw, and other beasts, as appeared by their tracks, as also divers fowls, as cranes, hernshaws, bitterns, geese, mallards, teals, and other fowls, in great plenty; also great store of peas, which grow in certain plots all the island over. (148–49)

Further exploration and investigation in the area quite convinced Brereton that he had found paradise on earth, for, compared with Cape Cod and its islands, "the most fertile part of all England is (of itself) but barren" (152).

The English had no trouble with the Native Americans, with whom they feasted. The Indians liked all of the white man's food except the mustard, "whereat they made many a sour face" (154). Thereafter, the two parties traded freely, with the English receiving an abundance of fruits. When they finally departed, the Indians "made huge cries and shouts of joy unto us, and we, with our trumpet and cornet and casting up our caps into the air, made them the best farewell we could" (157). Though Brereton called the Indians savages, he wrote favorably of their strength of body and their wit, for which he credited the climate; he remarked that even though the English stayed there but a short time, the men "were much fatter and in better health than when we went out of England" (159). The original expectation had been that a group of voyagers would remain to establish claim to the lands; but, when some of them changed their minds, it was decided that all of the men would be needed for the return trip. Thus, the first Englishmen to visit New England left "with as many true sorrowful eyes as were before desirous to see it" (159). They brought back to England a cargo of sassafras roots, then considered valuable medicinally.

The report of Gosnold's voyage by Brereton was published through the good offices of Richard Hakluyt, who was always looking for propaganda. Other supporting documents were also included in the pamphlet, and in a second edition—indicating that the voyage was of considerable interest—appeared "Inducements to the liking of the voyage intending toward Virginia" (180), another aspect of Hakluyt's continuing campaign to colonize America.

A Colony in Maine

Gosnold's voyage and the published report of it did prepare the way for other voyages, an important one being under the command of George Waymouth; it was well reported by James Rosier, who may have been a Roman Catholic priest, in *A True Relation of the most prosperous voyage made this present yeere 1605 by Captaine George Waymouth, in the Discovery of the Land of Virginia* (1605). (In its earliest stages, the plan was that the colonists would be English Catholic gentlemen, their tenants, and Catholic refugees who had left England.)[27]

Brereton's and Rosier's reports provide the only publicity for "Northern Virginia" before Captain John Smith's *Description of New England* (1616). David and Alison Quinn have shown that Rosier's work "stands in time at a crucial point in English concern . . . with eastern North America as a whole."[28] This account is a literate, interesting work, though it lacks the excitement and sense of discovery of Brereton's report on Cape Cod. Like Hariot, Rosier had taken careful notes; indeed, he wrote that he had been employed specifically to "make true report of the discovery" (251), and one can see that he did his work well. The publication of his report was delayed for a brief time, he observed, until plans were completed for a colony to be established in the area. (The plans, under Roman Catholic auspices, collapsed as a result of the Gunpowder Plot, late in 1605.) Rosier made the location of the site obscure to prevent "some foreign nation" from gaining "some knowledge of the place" (252).

Though George Waymouth, the leader of Rosier's company, may have intended to make Narragansett Bay his destination, winds drove the ship farther north after Nantucket had been sighted. The area they inadvertently visited proved to be as fruitful as the more southern area. They first landed at what was probably Monhegan Island (Maine), and while some men went ashore, others found that codfish and haddock were abundant. They found a harbor that they liked so much that they called it Pentecost Harbor. What is today called St. George's Harbor they found was not only a "good harbor (which is an excellent comfort) but because every day we did more and more discover the pleasant fruitfulness, insomuch as many of our company wished themselves settled here, not expecting any further hopes or discovery to be made" (266).

The explorers soon made contact with the Indians, whom they admired for their "exceeding good invention, quick understanding, and ready capacity" (269). While the English feared the Indians' treachery, probably with good reason, the Indians were also dubious about the English, who pretended to be interested only in trading. "We victualled them and gave them aqua vitae [brandy], which they tasted but would by no means drink; our beverage [beer or cider] they liked well. We gave them sugar candy, which after they had tasted they liked and desired more" (272). Having made a great show of friendliness, the English were in a position to take captives, "a matter of great importance for the full accomplishment of our voyage." They "shipped five savages, two canoes, with all their bows and arrows" (284–85). The English do not seem to have considered this kidnapping cause for the Indians to distrust them, for Rosier reported that "we used the people with as great kindness as we could devise or found them capable of." The reason was self-interest: "we found the land a place answerable to the interest of our discovery, viz., fit for any nation to inhabit" (272–73).

Much of Rosier's *True Relation* is a report about the Indians, for curiosity about them was great. When one of the Englishmen spent a night with them, he was able to describe a religious ceremony he had witnessed. It began when a leader, in the midst of a gathering of his people, stood and,

looking about suddenly cried with a loud voice, "Baugh Waugh." Then the women fall down and lie upon the ground. And the men all together answering the same, fall a stamping round about the fire with both feet, as hard as they can, making the ground shake, with sundry outcries and change of voice and sound. Many take the firesticks and thrust them into the earth, and then rest awhile. Of a sudden beginning as before, they continue stamping till the younger sort fetched from the shore many stones, of which every man took one, and first beat

upon them with their firesticks, then with the stones beat the earth with all their
strength.(278)

The cry "Baugh Waugh," in the form of "pow-wow" became a name for
such ceremonies.

Rosier's work is full of notes intended to demonstrate the usefulness of
the area as a site for a colony. Particularly attractive to the explorers
was the St. George's River, which they considered incomparable, finer
than the Orinoco, according to some of the party who had seen it with Sir
Walter Raleigh. It was "the most rich, beautiful, large, and secure-
harboring river the world affordeth" (293). Even hunger could not keep
the explorers from continuing up the river, not because they needed to
know more about it but because they could not deny themselves the
pleasure of seeing its beauty. Like Brereton and later Captain John
Smith, Rosier saw New England at its summer best. Those who spent a
winter there had a different story to tell.

This voyage, Rosier's account, and the five Indians whom the explorers brought back with them from what is now Maine created much
interest in a settlement in the north of "Virginia." The Indians' presence
stimulated further interest in colonization. Ferdinando Gorges wrote
that the exhibition of the kidnapped Indians "must be acknowledged the
means under God of putting on foot and giving life to all our plantations."[29] Gorges and Sir John Popham, the Lord Chief Justice, planned a
permanent colony in Maine on the Sagadahoc (later called Kennebec)
River. (Raleigh had now lost his rights in North America.) Though a
substantial group of colonists was sent out in 1607, six months after the
Jamestown settlers had left, the place where they intended to settle was
wholly unsuitable for agriculture. Moreover, the Northern group found
the Maine winter too severe and returned to England in 1608.[30]

William Strachey

One of the best reports of a voyage to America from a literary point of
view was written by William Strachey, who was bound for Virginia in
1609 when his ship, carrying Sir Thomas Gates and Sir George Somers,
was wrecked in the Bermudas. Gates was on his way to be successor to
Captain John Smith as governor of the Virginia colony; Somers was
admiral of a flotilla of seven ships and two pinnaces, carrying 600
colonists. Strachey's party survived and thus were more fortunate than

those who were not shipwrecked and went on to Virginia, for there few of the latter survived the difficult winter.

A True Reportory of the Wrack and Redemption of Sir Thomas Gates, Knight, upon and from the Islands of the Bermudas is an extended account of the Bermuda and Virginia adventures by a man who served as secretary of the Virginia colony's governing council.[31] Later Strachey also wrote *The Historie of Travell into Virginia Britannia*. Neither work was published in his lifetime—the latter, indeed, not until the nineteenth century. *A True Reportory* was first published in 1625, when Samuel Purchas included it in *Purchas His Pilgrimes*, Purchas being Hakluyt's successor. (Purchas's work is discussed below.) Strachey's work seems to have circulated widely before 1625 in manuscript, as is evidenced by the fact that William Shakespeare drew on it for the writing of *The Tempest*.[32] What interested Shakespeare was Strachey's description of the storm that led to the wreck. Another admirer was the nineteenth-century critic Moses Coit Tyler, who found that some sentences in it, "for imagination and pathetic beauty, for vivid implications of appalling danger and disaster, can hardly be surpassed in the whole range of English prose."[33]

Strachey's ship had begun to leak badly at the very beginning of the storm, and much of the description deals with the efforts to locate the leak and prevent the ship from sinking.

There might be seen master, master's mate, boatswain, quartermaster, coopers, carpenters, and who not, with candles in their hands, creeping along the ribs viewing the sides, searching every corner, and listening in every place if they could hear the water run. Many a weeping leak was this way found and hastily stopped, and at length one in the gunner room made up with I know not how many pieces of beef. But all was to no purpose; the leak (if it were but one) which drunk in our greatest seas and took our destruction fastest could not then be found, nor ever was, by any labor, counsel, or search. The waters still increasing and the pumps going, which at length choken with bringing up whole and continual biscuit (and indeed all we had, ten thousand weight), it was conceived as most likely that the leak might be sprung in the bread room; whereupon the carpenter went down and ripped up all the room but could not find it so. (8–9)

In the meanwhile, "It could not be said to rain; the waters like whole rivers did flood in the air" (7). The wind blew the ship "at all adventures, sometimes north and northeast, then north and by west, and in an instant again varying two or three points, and sometimes half the compass" (13).

At last Somers saw land, after four days and three nights of storm, but the land was the infamous Devils' Islands, believed to be "no habitation for men but rather given over to the devils and wicked spirits" (16). Though Strachey found the islands pleasanter than their reputation suggested, he was not much impressed with this area. Presumably, the frustration of being unable to get to Virginia, his destination, made him blind to the many virtues of the islands. (A different view of the Bermudas was provided in 1613 by William Crashaw, who wrote that the unintended landing there was the work of God, who meant this paradise for the English.)[34] Strachey fairly reported, however, the rich supply of food that the islands provided: fish, fowl, wild hogs, turtles ("reasonable toothsome"); but the weather was unpleasant, especially the winter, which was "heavy and melancholy" (21).

Having built a ship, the *Deliverance*, Somers and his men found their way to Jamestown, where they discovered immense "wants and wretchedness" (67) among the colonists despite the richness of the land. New arrivals and those who had survived the winter all felt that they had no choice but to abandon Virginia. They had made plans to leave when reinforcements and supplies arrived. Strachey ends his *True Reportory* with a brief account of life in Jamestown and later events there.

Strachey's longer work, *The Historie of Travell into Virginia Britannia*, was written between about 1609 and 1612, though not published until 1849.[35] It is much like Smith's *Generall Historie* in that it is largely a compilation of other men's writings, with some additions based on the author's experiences in Virginia. Strachey made extensive use of Smith's portion of *A Map of Virginia*; in fact, he borrowed about four-fifths of it, without indicating—as Smith usually did—his indebtednesses.

Despite this similarity, Smith's and Strachey's books are very different. Strachey had studied at Cambridge University and was friendly with London members of the literary profession. Smith was much less well educated and was a soldier by profession. Something of Strachey's learning and art can be seen in the prefatory paragraph to his first chapter on the Indians:

It was not perhaps too curious a thing to demand how these people might come first, and from who, and whence, to inhabit these so far remote westerly parts of the world, having no intercourse with Asia, Africa, nor Europe, and considering the whole world, so many years, by all knowledge received, was supposed to be only contained and circumscribed in the discovered and travelled bounds of those three, according to that old conclusion in the school: "Quicquid praeter Africam, et Europam est, Asia est." Whatsoever land doth neither appertain unto Africa nor to Europe is part of Asia. As also to question how it should be, that they, if descended from the people of the first creation, should maintain so general and gross a defection from true knowledge of God, with one kind, as it were, of rude and savage life, customs, manners, and religion, it being to be granted that with us (infallibly) they had one and the same descent and beginning from the universal deluge, in the scattering of Noah's children and nephews with their families (as little colonies) some to one, some to other borders of the earth to dwell. (53)

Unfortunately Strachey did not write a history of the Virginia colony in 1609–11, when he was there; in fact, his *True Reportory* provides more information about events in Virginia than does his *Historie*. Instead, in preparing the *Historie*, Strachey supplemented Smith's reports on the land and its people. His borrowings from Smith begin with the very first paragraph of the *Historie*:

Smith	Strachey
Virginia is a country	Virginia Britannia is a country
in America that lieth	in America that lieth
between the degrees of 34 and	between the degrees of 30 and
44 of the north latitude,	44 of the north latitude,
the bounds thereof	the bounds whereof
	must be thus laid:
on the east side are	on the east runneth
the great ocean.	the great ocean
	or main Atlantic sea;
On the south lieth Florida;	on the south lieth Florida;
on the north, Nova Francia.	on the north, Nova Francia.
As the west thereof, the	As the west thereof, the
limits are unknown. Of all	limits are unknown, only it
this country we purpose not	is supposed there may be
to speak, but only of that	found the descent into the
part which was planted by	South Sea, by the Spaniards
the Englishmen in the year of	called Mar del sur, so
our Lord 1606. (47)	meeting on the backside (as
	it were) of us with that
	doubtful Northwest Passage
	which leads into the east to
	China, Cathay, Japan. . . . (31)

Borrowing like this by a writer of Strachey's talent strikes one as strange indeed.

Strachey's work is a fragment, perhaps because his efforts at publication received no encouragement. What he left is valuable, though it is not what the title suggests, a history of Virginia. The *Historie* is in two books. The first is devoted to a description of Virginia and its people; the second begins the story of voyages to America but gets no further than the story of the colony at Sagadahoc. Because Strachey did not have it published, the *Historie* did not contribute to interest in Virginia, but its format is helpful in understanding the similar shape of Smith's *Generall Historie*.

Hakluyt and Purchas

While Virginia's indebtedness to Richard Hakluyt is not fully known, that propagandist for colonization was probably more responsible than any other man for the continuing interest in colonization. It is natural to find him among the patentees of the London Virginia Company in 1606. He seems to have been expected to serve the colony as chaplain, but perhaps he was too old to make the trip. In the critical year 1609, when the colony was in desperate straits, he translated from the Portuguese an account of DeSoto's explorations in southeastern North America. Entitled *Virginia Richly Valued by the description of the mainland of Florida her next neighbor*, the work was dedicated to the Virginia Company: the book was said to "yield much light to our enterprise now on foot." Hakluyt also published *Nova Francia, or the description of that part of New France which is one continent with Virginia* (1609), which was expected to provide "greater encouragement . . . to prosecute that generous and goodly action," the colonizing of America, according to the preface.[36] Again publication was connected with colonization.

Hakluyt's work was carried on by a successor, a man whose career and that of John Smith touched at several points. According to Eva G. R. Taylor, Smith was Samuel Purchas's most important friend.[37] Purchas was, like Hakluyt, a clergyman. He began his publishing career in 1613, when a substantial folio volume appeared entitled *Purchas His Pilgrimage*, a history of religion with considerable emphasis on geography. Purchas found the collections of Hakluyt particularly useful, as he acknowledged; as a result Hakluyt supplied him with manuscripts that he used in the second edition of the *Pilgrimage* in 1614.

After Hakluyt's death, Purchas obtained (on "hard conditions," he noted) Hakluyt's papers.[38] With them and his own collections he prepared *Hakluytus Posthumus, or Purchas His Pilgrimes*. (The *Pilgrimes* is sometimes confused with the earlier *Pilgrimage*.) Though Purchas was the successor to Hakluyt, his work was distinctly different from that of the great Elizabethan. Hakluyt was a collector of documents that he had sought out or had prepared: he compiled archives. Purchas wrote a history of travel and exploration, portions of which are documents and accounts by others, usually in abridged form or excerpted.[39] Purchas wanted to provide a readable book. (He was doubtless influenced by the fact that King James had read the *Pilgrimage* seven times.) He avoided all that he considered tedious, and, though historians are appalled by the editing that was a consequence, Samuel Taylor Coleridge in "Kubla Khan" shows that the book long retained its attractiveness. (Coleridge, it will be recalled, was reading Purchas one day in 1797 when he fell asleep; when he awoke, he found that the poem "Kubla Khan" wrote itself.)[40] Like Hakluyt, Purchas was a propagandist for American colonization; he considered it a work pleasing to God.

Purchas and Captain John Smith may well have known each other before Smith went to Virginia, and Smith assisted in the preparation of the *Pilgrimage* of 1613. Purchas in turn helped Smith in the preparation of the *Generall Historie* by permitting him to use materials that were to appear in the *Pilgrimes*.[41] Hakluyt's and Purchas's works also served as models for Smith in the preparation of his *Generall Historie*. One other aspect of the relationship should be mentioned: Smith provided an account of his own travels in Hungary and Russia for the *Pilgrimes*.

Travel, discovery, reports, propaganda, and colonization are closely connected in the story of English travellers in the days of Elizabeth I and James I. It was not enough for men of adventure to discover "virgin lands" across the sea. It took the writings of men such as Hakluyt, Hariot, Raleigh, and Smith to inspire men who had remained at home with a vision of these lands and of the possibilities that awaited them there. This literature of travel and exploration had a great impact on England and, indeed, the world. If the discovery of the New World was the most important event in the history of the Old World, the reason was to a considerable extent this literature and its fruits. The promotion pamphlet in particular is, as Louis B. Wright states, "a form of literature not often noted by critics but perhaps of greater significance than poetry or the novel upon the quality of our civilization."[42]

Chapter Two

The Place of Writing in the Life of Captain John Smith

John Smith's published writings are eight in number; a modern edition fills three substantial volumes. But only one of the eight can really be regarded as a book. Four are pamphlets of fewer than 50 pages, one of them—the first version of *New Englands Trials*—being a mere 20 pages. A *Map of Virginia* is not a small book, but Smith's contribution consti- tutes only the first third, fewer than 40 pages, and perhaps the first two chapters of the 12 chapters of the second part, *The Proceedings of the English Colonie in Virginia*.

Furthermore, Smith's one real book, the *Generall Historie*, includes a reprinting, with only small changes and additions, of his portion of *A Map of Virginia* (Book II), his *A Description of New England*, and his *New Englands Trials* (Book V)—in all, about a fifth of the whole. Of the remainder of the *Generall Historie*, little is new. Book I is a collection of travel accounts edited by Smith, Book IV is mostly compilation, and Book V is a history of the Bermudas compiled mostly from one source. Even the most famous portion of the *Generall Historie*, Book III, the story of Smith's adventures in Virginia, is a revision of the account published in *The Proceedings*, a report in which Smith's contribution was not major. Smith did indeed add to Book III a good many pages, including a few that tell the familiar story of his rescue by Pocahontas. The *Generall Historie* was for 200 years and more of real value as a compilation made by a knowledgeable authority. It contains occasional fresh pages of com- ment and historical writing. But it is scarcely an original work. Never- theless, the preparation of the *General Historie* took time and effort, perhaps a year and a half. In contrast, *A Description of New England* was written quickly in 1615 while Smith was captive aboard the *Don de Dieu*, a French corsair.

Facts of Publication

Smith began his writing career fortuitously, for his first publication, *A True Relation of such occurrences and accidents of noate as hath hapned in*

Virginia since the first planting of that Collony (1608), was based on a letter written to an acquaintance in England; it was definitely not intended for publication. His second work might be called an occasional piece, for *A Map of Virginia* (1612) was intended to counteract what Smith and his friends considered to be false reports. Although Smith seems to have found his proper medium with *A Description of New England* (1616), a mixture of reporting and propaganda, he wrote in the next few years only one other work of this sort, *New England's Trials* (1620; enlarged 1622). Two of his last works give the impression of having been written for profit: *An Accidence Or The Pathway to Experience, Necessary for Young Seamen* (1626), revamped and augmented as *A Sea Grammar, With the Plaine Exposition of Smith's Accidence for young Sea-men, enlarged* (1627); and *The True Travels* (1630), an account of Smith's pre–Virginia adventures, published in part by Samuel Purchas in 1625. *Advertisements For the unexperienced Planters of New England, or any where, Or, the Path-way to experience to erect a Plantation* (1631), one of Smith's most impressive works, is a kind of valediction, though in it he wrote that he was then working on a history of the sea. Presumably he did not finish it; he died that same year, and the work is not extant.

These facts of publication suggest that Smith was a man who turned to writing only occasionally except for the period when he prepared the *Generall Historie*. What Smith otherwise did in the years between 1617, when his final plans to return to America were frustrated (he did not stop hoping to go), and his death in 1631, is known only hazily. His biographers have pieced together what little information is found, mostly concerning the circumstances surrounding the publication of his work and his known associates in these last years. But the account of these 14 years fills only 58 pages of Barbour's authoritative biography, and must of the material is tangential. A little more information has recently come to light from the discovery of complimentary poems published in the books of other writers. One was John Taylor, the "water poet," for whose *Armado* (1627) Smith wrote a poem. (Smith calls Taylor his friend.) Smith's poems underscore what similar poems by others in Smith's work indicate: that he had a good many friends with at least some literary pretensions. The place of writing in Smith's life would be easier to ascertain if more were known, for example, about the circumstances surrounding the composition of *The True Travels*. From what facts are available about Smith's life it is clear that writing was, as Bradford Smith stated, "not his life but a substitute for living." [1]

Who Touches This Book, Touches a Man

Until 1617, when he was 37, Smith's life had been very full. He had been a soldier in the Netherlands and in Hungary; he had toured France, Italy, the Mediterranean, Russia, Central Europe, and North Africa; he had been enslaved in Turkey and Tartary—all before he was 25. As late as 1628, Smith considered himself not a writer but a soldier, as is indicated by his poem on Robert Norton's *The Gunner Shewing the Whole Practice of Artillery*: "We soldiers to embrace / This rare and useful work." (Smith signed the poem "Captain John Smith, Hungarienses.") In the preface to the *Generall Historie* he excused his writing on the grounds that "The style of a soldier is not eloquent, but honest and justifiable" (II, 44).

Soon after his return from his foreign adventures, Smith was a participant in the early stages of planning the Virginia colony, was made one of the seven councilors appointed to govern the colony, took a crucial role in the colony's early activities, was made president of the governing council, and was back in England less than three years after he had left. These were the years Smith liked to remember. The years from his return in 1609 through 1617 are less fully known, but much time can be accounted for: preparing two publications, making a trip to New England, and planning two other voyages to America, both of which miscarried. After 1617, he waited impatiently for another chance for adventure.

Because his life was an exciting and frustrating one, Smith's writings reflect in the most direct possible manner his own activities, which are referred to even in unlikely places, with the result that his writings appear to many readers to be egotistical. Thus, *Advertisements For the unexperienced Planters of New England* includes a chapter on "My first voyage to new England, my return, and profit." Smith justified his personal approach, for he noted in the *Generall Historie*, "Had I not discovered and lived in the most of those parts, I could not possibly have collected the substantial truth from such a number of variable relations . . ." (II, 44). He protested, "I am no compiler by hearsay, but have been a real actor; I take myself to have a property in them" (II, 41). After 1616, Smith's writings reveal a damaged ego. He found that he could not be objective, for his frustrations were always with him. Thus, Smith's life and works are not discrete; his works reflect his life. Because they were interwoven—all of his writings are at least partly autobiographical—the reader of his works and this study will find it useful to have an overview of Smith's life. Particularly important are the Virginia years, to which Smith frequently referred in his writings.

Smith's Early Years

In the late sixteenth century, English society was not static; John Smith's father, a Lincolnshire farmer, was able to rise significantly in the social scale. By the end of his life, he owned a brick house and farm animals and household goods listed as worth £78, perhaps $25,000 today. An inventory cites, for example:

Item: one feather bed, a bolster, a blanket, a covering, and two pillows.
        23 shillings
Item: two pewter candlesticks, four brass candlesticks, three salts, two pewter cups, one tun, and a bowl of pewter, one pewter basin, and a chafing dish
                                          13 shilling, 4 pence[2]

Smith's father owned his own farm and two sizable pieces of land. His was "the biggest house in Willoughby" and "without parallel in the country round about"; he was "gentry in all but title."[3] Had our Smith taken up his father's occupation, he might have been successful enough to claim the title of gentleman as a routine matter.[4] Instead, John Smith won the title by a more adventurous process. His father could have called himself a yeoman, but in his will he preferred to name himself as simply a poor tenant of Lord Willoughby, the lord of the manor.[5] With such a background, John Smith was inevitably class-conscious and ambitious.

Smith's education took place in the school of the neighboring town of Alford and later at Louth, not far away, where he was presumably a boarder. In his autobiography, Smith wrote merely that he had been "a scholar in the two free schools of Alford and Louth" (III, 153). He must have started school about age six and continued until he was 15; many students left at that age. The basis of his studies was Latin, with a good deal of emphasis on grammar and later on composition.[6] Very little of this learning shows in his writings, in which he carefully avoided any Latin phrases, unlike most writers of the time. (He did show some knowledge of ancient history.)

But, even as a teenager, "his mind being even then set upon brave adventures" (III, 153–54), Smith was determined to go to sea. His father, willing for him to leave school, was not willing for him to run off to seek his fortune. Instead, he arranged for him to serve as an apprentice. Smith's own account of his activities at this time is confused, but the general outline of events can at least be made out. Off he went to King's

Lynn, some 65 miles away, to work for Thomas Sendall, a highly successful merchant. The elder Smith presumably felt that his son's zeal for adventure might be satisfied by the thought that eventually he could travel abroad on Sendall's behalf. But the younger Smith insisted on going to sea immediately, and Sendall was unwilling. Soon after his father's death in 1596, the 16-year-old abandoned his apprenticeship. Again the facts are unclear, but this was probably the time when Smith began to be his own master. He went to the Netherlands, where he began his career as a soldier. There he served three or four years. Obviously this was the kind of apprenticeship he preferred.

In 1599, Smith was back in England, ready for more adventures. He managed to be taken on as a servant by Lord Willoughby's younger son, who was about to tour France. Smith got as far as Orleans before he was sent home. Then occurred a minor but characteristic adventure. Smith decided to spend some time in France, where he was befriended by David Hume, a Scotsman. Hume borrowed money from Smith, who received in return letters recommending him to the court of King James of Scotland. Off he went to seek his fortune there. Though delayed by shipwreck he found his way to Scotland, but to no avail. Perhaps to get some perspective, Smith returned home. There he read and learned a good deal about horseback riding. His teacher, a descendant of the last emperor of the Eastern Roman Empire,[7] seems to have given him ideas about adventuring to that part of the world. Already, at age 20, Smith was a much traveled, self-reliant soldier of fortune.

Smith's next series of adventures is the subject of his autobiography; they are best treated in connection with that strange book, *The True Travels* (see chapter 7). Here it is enough to say that for four and a half years, Smith toured France, Italy, Greece, the Balkans, Austria, Poland, and Germany; fought in the wars between the Hungarians and the Turks; was captured and sent to Constantinople, then to the Caucasus, where he escaped. Before returning home, he also toured North Africa. He ended these adventures having made a name for himself. He had been made captain (and entitled a gentleman) and thus escaped the anonymity of being called simply John Smith.

Smith in Virginia

In 1605, Smith had in no way satisfied his taste for adventure. He next intended, he later noted, to go to Guiana to join the English colony there: "I should have been a party" (III, 224). Instead, he somehow became identified with a group of men planning a trip to North America to establish a new colony.[8] Smith seems to have known little about the backers of the venture; later, when he was in Virginia and responsible to them, he was extremely unsympathetic with their demands. The men Smith came to know at this time were the leaders of the group who came to America: Captain Bartholomew Gosnold, whose voyage to Cape Cod in 1602 had been attractively written up by John Brereton; Edwin Maria Wingfield, a well-born former soldier in his forties; and Christopher Newport, a highly experienced seaman who was to conduct the colonists to Virginia and later bring over supplies. Smith probably also talked with Thomas Hariot, who had written about his year with the Roanoke colony in North Carolina. Very little is known about how Smith became identified with the group; he himself explained in the *Generall Historie* that he had invested more than £500 in the undertaking (II, 326). (According to one version of his European adventures, he had returned to England with 1,000 ducats, about £500.)[9] The records indicate that Smith's subscription to the Virginia colony was £9.

Before the colonists left, they received elaborate instructions from the group that sponsored them, the Virginia Company of London.[10] The officers of the colonists carefully followed these "Instructions," though the consequences were often undesirable. For example, the site of the colony, Jamestown, was an extremely unhealthy place, and many colonists died as a result; but the location was what the instructions called for. Smith was not happy to be obliged to follow directions prepared by men remote from the place where decisions had to be made, yet he, too, often found that he had no other choice. The colonists were even compelled to look for a northwest passage to the Pacific Ocean. Among the most important "Instructions" were the following:

When it shall please God to send you on the coast of Virginia, you shall do your best endeavor to find out a safe port in the entrance of some navigable river, making choice of such a one as runneth farthest into the land, and if you happen to discover divers portable [navigable] rivers, and amongst them any one that hath two main branches, if the difference be not great make choice of that which bendeth toward the northwest, for that way you shall soonest find the other sea. . . .

. . . You must observe if you can whether the river on which you plant doth spring out of mountains or out of lakes. If it be out of any lake, the passage to the other sea will be more easy, and it is like enough that out of the same lake you shall find some spring which run the contrary way towards the East India Sea, for the great and famous rivers of Volga, Tanais, and Dwina have three heads near joined, and yet the one falleth into the Caspian Sea, the other into the Euxine Sea, and the third into the Paelonian Sea.

In all your passages, you must have great care not to offend the naturals, if you can eschew it, and employ some few of your company to trade with them for corn and other lasting victuals. . . . [11]

The colonists thus were chiefly to be explorers seeking the legendary Northwest Passage.

In December 1606, a group of 105 colonists departed in three ships. Of these, at least 59 were "gentlemen" who could not be expected to work. The expedition traveled via the West Indies, where one colonist died from the heat. Smith had meanwhile been made prisoner by the leaders, presumably as a result of some disagreement. Arriving in April 1607, the colonists were briefly attacked by Indians until the Europeans indicated that their motives were friendly. They located a site, named it Jamestown, and began to fortify it. The ruling body was a group of seven men: Newport; Wingfield, who was elected president; Gosnold; Captain John Martin; Captain George Kendall; Captain John Ratcliffe; and Captain John Smith, no longer a prisoner but still one of the most obscure of the group. Smith was not for a time, however, permitted to serve; but when Captain Newport began an exploration of the James River, as the "Instructions" required, Smith was a member of the party. The journey up the James convinced Newport that the Pacific Ocean was only a little way farther.

By the time Smith was admitted to the governing council, several colonists had been killed by the Indians in both major attacks and minor skirmishes. On 22 June 1607, Newport and two ships returned to England, taking with them a letter from the six remaining members of the council that provides insight into the situation of the colonists, especially into one of the most serious problems they faced: the sailors of the supply ships, always ready for a quick profit, subverted the work of the settlers. The letter reads, in part:

Within less than seven weeks we are fortified well against the Indians, we have sown good store of wheat; we have sent you a taste of clapboard [used for making casks]; we have built some houses; we have spared some hands to a discovery; and still as God shall enable us with strength we will better and better our proceedings. Our easiest and richest commodity, being sassafras roots, were gathered up by the sailors with loss and spoil of many of our tools and with drawing of our men from our labor to their uses against our knowledge to our prejudices. We earnestly entreat you (and do trust) that you take such order as we be not in this thus defrauded, since they be all our waged men, yet do we wish that they be reasonably dealt withal so as all the loss neither fall on us nor them. I believe they have thereof two tons at the least, which if they scatter abroad at their pleasure will pull down our price a long time. This we leave to your wisdoms.[12]

Though food was in short supply after the departure of Newport, the colonists, instead of establishing themselves, did little, and the leaders disagreed among themselves. Before long, death began to thin out the ranks of the settlers rapidly; Captain Gosnold was among those to die. The troublesome Captain Kendall was removed from the council, reducing the number to four. In September, Wingfield was removed from command and from the council for incompetence by the remaining three, who elected Ratcliffe president. Smith became supply officer.

The adventures of the period from September 1607 to June 1608, including encounters with Powhatan, the Indian leader, are described in Smith's *A True Relation*, which he wrote at the end of this period (see chapter 3). By June, when Smith sent the letter that formed the basis of *A True Relation* to England (it was rushed to a departing ship), Wingfield and Martin had decided to return to home, and Smith's importance in the life of the colony was steadily growing. He led exploring missions on long trips up Chesapeake Bay during the summer; in September, when Ratcliffe's term expired, Smith was elected president.

Soon he found himself forced to follow new instructions prepared by the London backers of the colony, though they were—from Smith's point of view—very impractical. They included orders to crown Powhatan in order to encourage the Indian leader to be more subservient to the English. (The crowning took place but did not have the desired effect.) Smith was also expected to increase the shipment of lumber and other products of the colony to England, though the quantity of supplies coming to the colony from England was minimal, and the visiting sailors continued to create havoc with the colony's economy. Smith's chief problem was to obtain food for the colonists, now 200 in number. The Indians were the chief source of food, and increasingly force seemed required to obtain it from them. As a result, under Powhatan's leadership they became more and more combative. At several crucial times Pocahontas, Powhatan's daughter, came to the aid of Smith and the colonists.

But, in time, Smith's leadership had its effects: at last the colonists were put to work. According to *The Proceedings* published with *A Map of Virginia*,

Now we so quietly followed our business that in three months we made three or four last [about 40 barrels] of pitch, and tar, and soap ashes; produced a trial of glass; made a well in the fort of excellent sweet water, which till then was wanting; built some twenty houses; recovered our church; provided nets and weirs for fishing; (and to stop the disorders of our disorderly thieves and the savages) built a blockhouse in the neck of our isle, kept by a garrison, to entertain the savages' trade, and none to pass or repass, savage nor Christian, without the president's order. Thirty or forty acres of ground we digged and planted; of three sows in one year increased sixty and odd pigs, and near five hundred chickens brought up themselves (without having any meat given them); but the hogs were transported to Hog Isle, where also we built a blockhouse, with a garrison, to give us notice of any shipping, and for their [the lookouts'] exercise, they made clapboard, wainscot, and cut down trees against the ship's coming. (I,263)

All seemed to be going well when it was discovered that the grain that was stored for later use had rotted and been eaten by rats. As a result, work was stopped on all these projects, and everyone was set to work finding food. Furthermore, Smith had to struggle with Dutch and Swiss laborers who conspired with Powhatan and the Indians in attempts to destroy the colony.

Meanwhile, the Virginia Company had decided to make a larger effort to support and develop the Jamestown colony. Sir Thomas Gates was named head of the colony, to be succeeded by Lord de la Warr; and many colonists were enrolled. A whole fleet of ships started out for Virginia. But the flagship of the fleet, captained by Newport and with Gates and Sir George Somers—Gates's deputy—aboard, was shipwrecked in the Bermudas. (The shipwreck was vividly described by William Strachey; see chapter 1.) When the remaining colonists arrived in Virginia, Smith had the responsibility of a command now much increased, including many women and children. Because of the food shortage, he divided the colonists into a number of what were supposed to be self-sustaining groups. He also had the additional problem of dealing with the leaders among the recently arrived colonists, some of whom felt that, until Gates arrived, someone else, not Smith, should govern.

Smith was facing the most trying circumstances of his Virginia years. It was early September, and he knew that his days as president were very limited, but much work had to be done before the winter came. He therefore visited the group of colonists who were making a base at the falls of the James River, 100 miles from Jamestown. Having done what he could for the group, who were on the verge of mutiny, Smith started out for Jamestown. The 1612 *Proceedings* describes the next events. "[Smith] Sleeping in his boat . . . one accidentally fired his powder bag, which tore his flesh from his body and thighs nine or ten inches square, in a most pitiful manner, but to quench the tormenting fire, frying him in his clothes, he leaped over board into the deep river, where ere they could recover him, he was near drowned. In this estate, without either chirurgeon or chirurgery, he was to go near one hundred miles [to Jamestown]" (I, 272). Because Smith's accident completely incapacitated him, he left Virginia for England in October, 1609. Though many found fault with his government and sent charges against him back to England, he was much missed by the colonists. Before the winter was over, the misruled colony was barely surviving; and Jamestown would have been abandoned had not Lord de la Warr and fresh supplies arrived. In the winter after Smith left, all but about 60 of the colonists died. Had Gates and Somers arrived as planned, and Smith not been injured, Smith would not have continued as president of the council but would no doubt have had an important post, that of defense officer of the colony. Later, when he sought to return to Virginia after the Indians had massacred the settlers, it was a military post such as this one that he wanted.

Smith and New England

Back in England, Smith found a new friend and supporter in Edward Seymour, Earl of Hertford. Except for this fact, next to nothing is known about the next few years of his life. He prepared a description of Virginia, published in 1612 as part of *A Map of Virginia*, along with a narrative of Virginia events of 1607–10, to which he contributed (see chapter 4). Meanwhile the Virginia colony was barely surviving. Presumably as a consequence, Smith's attention strayed. He became interested in the area north of Virginia and in 1614 was given charge of two ships to sail to the Maine coast, often visited by English ships. Smith went there, as he later wrote, "to take whales and make trials of a mine of gold and copper. If those failed, fish and furs was then our refuge, to make ourselves savers howsoever" (I, 323). Smith later told the story of this important voyage in *A Description of New England* (1616) (see chapter 8).

After this voyage, Smith met Sir Ferdinando Gorges, an active member of the trading organization known as the Plymouth Company and a sponsor of the Sagadahoc colony, which had wintered on the Maine coast in 1607–8.[13] According to his 1616 pamphlet, Smith was assured by Gorges "and some others" that he would "have the managing [of] their authority in those parts during my life," and so he engaged himself "to undertake it for them" (I, 352).

Gorges and Smith planned a colony in New England: Gorges with difficulty found the financial support needed, and Smith was placed in charge of a small group of settlers. Two ships set out, but Smith's ship, the larger of the two, soon proved unseaworthy, and he was forced to return to England. In a smaller ship, Smith started out again but after a series of misadventures found his ship's officers unwilling to continue; they left Smith on a French pirate ship and departed. Only with great difficulty did he escape and find his way back to England.

Smith's bad luck must have been obvious to the cautious Gorges, but he had committed himself to Smith, who clearly was experienced with the New World. (This experience was manifested when Pocahontas, now married to John Rolfe, came to England in 1616; Smith reported her good qualities to the Queen.)[14] The persistent Smith finally had another chance to go to America. In the spring of 1617, he was given three ships and a small group of colonists to begin a colony in New England. Smith probably expected to go to Massachusetts, but for three months he and his ships waited, wind-bound, in Plymouth Harbor. Then, as Smith explained in 1620, "the season being past, the ships went for Newfoundland, whereby my design was frustrate, which was to me and my friends no small loss" (I, 399). This was the last time that Smith began an adventure westward. What connection he and Gorges had after this time is not known.

Years of Frustration and Writing

Throughout the remainder of his life Smith tried again and again to find sponsors for a colony in America. He sought support from Sir Francis Bacon in 1618; he published two pleas for support, one in 1620 and another in 1622 (see chapter 9); and he urged the London guilds to help him. He wanted to guide the "Pilgrims" who settled at Plymouth; instead they used his book and his map of New England. Seeking money in 1621, Smith cited his work for the Jamestown colony. In 1622, he asked the Virginia Company to send him to discipline the Indians. Always he sought in vain.

In 1622, Captain John Smith began his *Generall Historie*. It was to be a big book, by far Smith's longest. In 1623, he published a prospectus of the work to attract contributors, for printing would be expensive; he finally found a sponsor in the widow of the Earl of Hertford, who had aided him more than ten years before. She was now Duchess of Richmond and Lenox, and to her Smith dedicated *The Generall Historie of Virginia, New-England, and the Summer Isles*, published in 1624 (see chapters 4 and 5).

The book itself is unusually handsome. It includes a full-page portrait of the Duchess and another of Pocahontas; an elaborately engraved title page with portraits of Elizabeth I, James I, and Prince Charles, a map of the American coast from North Carolina to Maine, two coats of arms (the one granted Smith by Zsigmond Bathory and another possibly from the Smith family of Lincolnshire), and much more. Four folded maps are included: Ould Virginia (North Carolina), Virginia, the Summer Isles (the Bermudas), and New England. The first of these, occupying two pages, is illustrated with engravings derived from John White's drawings as reproduced by Theodore de Bry, and others depicting episodes from Smith's Virginia adventures, including his rescue by Pocahontas. The New England map includes a portrait of Smith at age 37. The book ought to be seen, though a good idea of its distinction can be gained from the Barbour edition, wherein the originals are somewhat reduced in size.

In the preparation of his *Generall Historie*, Smith worked with Samuel Purchas, who later published a brief account by Smith of his adventures from 1596 to 1604 in *Purchas His Pilgrimes* (1625) (see chapter 7). But these last years of Smith's are little known, except for the fact that in 1626 he published, apparently as a money-making venture, *An Accidence Or The Pathway to The Experience, Necessary for Young Seamen*, augmented in 1627 as *A Sea Grammar, With the Plaine Exposition of Smiths Accidence for young Sea-men, enlarged*, and that in 1627 and 1628 he wrote poems of commendation (see chapter 6).

It is known that Smith was keeping alert to developments in America, for in his continuation to the *Generall Historie* he reported on what had happened there since 1624. This account appeared in 1630 as the second part of Smith's *True Travels*, the augmented version of his autobiography. His interest in colonies is also shown by his last and best work, *Advertisements For the unexperienced Planters of New England* (1631) (see chapter 8). Smith's interest in America still stemmed from his conviction that he was responsible for the existence of the English colonies in America. He explained in the preface to *An Accidence*, "that the most of those fair plantations did spring from the fruits of my adventures and discoveries is evident" (III, 13).

A little glimpse of Smith's last days is provided by his comment in *Advertisements For the unexperienced Planters of New England* that he was writing in the house of "that worthy knight Sir Humphrey Mildmay, . . . in Essex in the parish of Danbury" (III, 289). Mildmay, a royalist gentleman, was connected by marriage with Smith's friend and landlord, Robert Bertie, Lord Willoughby de Eresbury.

On 21 June 1631, Captain John Smith died, leaving neither wife nor children—except for the American colonies, which were both to him, or so he wrote. His will deeded his Lincolnshire property to Thomas Packer, who in turn was to pay various benefactions. Including the cost of his funeral, these totaled £40. His epitaph was a fitting one.

> Here lies one conquered that hath conquered kings,
> Subdu'd large territories, and done things
> Which to the world impossible would seem
> But that the truth is held in more esteem.
> Shall I report his former service done
> In honor of his God and Christendom?
> How that he did divide from pagans three
> Their heads and lives, types of his chivalry,
> For which great service in that climate done
> Brave Sigismundus (King of Hungarion)
> Did give him as a coat of arms to wear
> Those conquered heads got by his sword and spear?
> Or shall I tell of his adventure since,
> Done in Virginia, that large continent?
> How that he subdued kings unto his yoke,
> And made those heathen fly, as wind doth smoke
> And made their land, being of so large a station,
> A habitation for our Christian nation,
> Where God is glorified, their wants supplied
> Which else for necessaries might have died?
> But what avails his conquests, now he lies
> Interr'd in earth, a prey for worms and flies?
> O! May his soul in sweet Elisium sleep,
> Until the keeper that all souls doth keep,
> Return to judgment, and that after thence,
> With angels he may have his recompense.
> (*Works*, III, 390)

Chapter Three
The Reporter

Captain John Smith supplied two kinds of reports on his Virginia years: one narrative, the other chiefly expository. He told the story of his first year in Virginia in *A True Relation* (1608), the first of his writings to be published. Smith's *True Relation* is the only consecutive narrative concerning Virginia that is wholly his, but he later contributed to an account, written mostly by others, of his whole two and a half years' stay in Virginia. Because he did not prepare *A True Relation* for publication or see it through the press, the book is far from being the letter that he wrote. It is marred by abruptnesses that are surely the result of passages being deleted. Nonetheless, *A True Relation* is fundamentally Smith's, and it is without question important.

The First American Book?

Histories of American literature traditionally begin with the year 1607, when the Jamestown colony began, or 1608, the date of what has been often called "the first American book." Not written as a book but as a letter to a friend in England, John Smith's *A True Relation of such occurrences and accidents of noate as hath hapned in Virginia since the first planting of that Collony* is the first English book written in America. Of course Thomas Hariot's literate and valuable *A brief and true report* of the Roanoke colony was published in 1588, but it had been written in England, as had the writing on New England of Brereton and Rosier. Other early accounts of Jamestown exist—by Captain Gabriel Archer, George Percy, and Captain Edward Maria Wingfield—but these were not in print as early as Smith's book; two of them, in fact, were not published until the nineteenth century.

The belief that anything that is to be called "American literature" must be written in English is subject to challenge, as is another criterion: that American literature is "literature written in any place that is now a part of the United States."[1] Such ideas are based on the concept that "America"—or more accurately the United States of America—is a unique place whose special character gives value for "Americans," more accurately citizens of the United States of America, to the literature (or to the art or music) that Americans have produced. Such work must somehow have an essential "Americanness." It is not clear why books written by Americans, for example, in Spanish should not have an American quality. Because these complex issues have not been resolved, we can conclude only that Smith's *A True Relation* has assumed an importance because *if* American literature began in Jamestown, as English-speaking Americans of the next 350 years believe, Smith's letter was made into the first American book.

Facts of Publication

A True Relation is a 44–page quarto pamphlet, "Written by Captain Smith, one of the said Collony, to a worshipfull friend of his in England"; and its running title is *Newes from Virginia*. It was written in early June 1608, and immediately thereafter sent to England. The author of the prefatory epistle, who signed himself "I. H." (perhaps John Healey, according to Philip L. Barbour, the editor of the best modern edition), explained that he came across the letter "by chance (as I take it, at the second or third hand)." The earliest printing did not identify the author by name, and the second misnamed him Thomas Watson. The author of the preface, along with others interested in the Virginia venture, judged that the letter should be published, "though it cannot be doubted that some faults escape in the printing, especially in the names of countries, towns, and peoples which are somewhat strange unto us." The preface writer then explains, tantalizingly, that "somewhat more" was written by Smith "which being as I thought (fit to be private) I would not adventure to make it public." These comments are misleading if they suggest that what we have is pretty much what Smith wrote. Philip Barbour describes Smith's letter as having been "ruthlessly edited and hastily and badly printed to an unusual degree." As a result, "the text of Smith's book remains in a sorry state" (I, 5, 6). Unlike the rest of Smith's writings published before 1624, *A True Relation* was not revised by its author and republished in *The Generall Historie of Virginia*. After the four printings of 1608, it was not reprinted until the nineteenth century.

A True Relation deals with the events of the first 13 months of the Jamestown colony, from 26 April 1607, when land was sighted, to the end of May 1608, when Smith's letter was sent via a ship returning to England that left on 2 June. It is a personal account, a letter, not a formal report for posterity, though Smith provided a fairly full description of the colony's adventures. His own exploits were of considerable importance during the period; and, even if Smith's personal bias is apparent, he was probably in the best position of any of the colonists to write this narrative summary. *A True Relation* is the raw material of history, not history itself; for Smith was too close to the events he described to discuss them in an appropriate perspective. At the beginning of the period with which he dealt, he was a minor figure among the colonists: for some unknown reason, perhaps his insubordination, he was under arrest for the first month or so of the settlement. But with remarkable rapidity, Smith's leadership virtues were recognized and he soon became the most important figure in the colony.

Struggles to Survive

After a heavily pruned account of the trip, Smith's letter begins with the arrival at Chesapeake Bay. The subject of *A True Relation* is the next 13 months. Though the period was marred by struggles for power, discontent, inertia, near-famine, disease, and threats from the Indians, the colonists did gain some knowledge of their environment, largely because of Smith's leadership. In early June 1607, Smith had been admitted to the governing council. In his position as supply officer (or "cape merchant"), a post he was given in September 1607, he had explored the Chickahominy River, a tributary of the James River, a few miles to the north.

Smith had little opportunity to explore merely for the sake of discovery, for the colonists were in desperate need of food. When the ships that had delivered them left in June, provisions were available for only 13 or 14 weeks. The Indians saved the day: when supplies were low, the settlers turned to them for sustenance. With many colonists already dead of famine and disease, Smith describes the situation when he became supply officer, five months after his arrival in America:

As at this time were most of our chiefest men either sick or discontented, the rest being in such despair as they would rather starve and rot with idleness than be persuaded to do anything for their own relief without constraint. Our victuals being now within eighteen days spent, and the Indians' trade decreasing, I was sent to the mouth of the [James] River to Kegquouhtan, an Indian town, to trade for corn and try the river for fish, but our fishing we could not effect by reason of the stormy weather. The Indians, thinking us near famished, with careless kindness offered us little pieces of bread and small handfuls of beans or wheat, for a hatchet or a piece of copper. In the like manner I entertained their kindness and in like scorn offered them like commodities, but the children, or any that showed extraordinary kindness, I liberally contented with free gift, such trifles as well contented them. (I, 35)

This early passage from Smith's first work shows the ironic tone that was to become almost characteristic and an awareness of the possibilities of verbal patterns, which unfortunately Smith never developed fully.

Captured by Indians

After a number of efforts, Smith was able to accumulate enough corn by bartering to permit him to make a trip in December mainly for exploration. With a small party of men, he went up the Chickahominy River much farther than he had been before, "towards Powhatan," the Indian emperor of whom the colonists had heard soon after their arrival in Virginia. This adventure and Smith's subsequent capture are probably the best-known events of his life, but the story constitutes less than one-fifth of *A True Relation* and does not mention Smith's memorable rescue by Pocahontas, to which he later frequently referred and which he described in his *Generall Historie*. These facts have made the earlier version less well known and at the same time, in the judgment of some readers, have demonstrated that the rescue in the later version is a fabrication.

Why the two accounts differ will never be known. Smith did note in 1608 that "So fat they fed me that I much doubted they intended to have sacrificed me to the *Quiyoughquosick*, which is a superior power they worship" (I, 59); but he described nothing like an execution scene, nor did he mention Pocahontas. Bradford Smith, who believed that Pocahontas did rescue Smith at this time, cited several reasons why he might have chosen to omit the story in 1608. The most persuasive one is that doing so would have hurt his reputation for bravery and subjected him to "leering remarks about his relations with the girl."[2] Philip Barbour, who also accepted the Pocahontas rescue story as true, thought that part of the account of Smith's captivity might have been suppressed as a horror story by the man who arranged the printing of the 1608 account.[3]

Because the trip was the occasion not only of Smith's capture but also of the death of two members of his group, he was quite defensive in his account of the adventure and justified his actions at some length. In all, he listed five factors that led him on when the river had become so narrow that he had to leave his barge and obtain a canoe to continue: (1) "the friendship of the Indians in conducting me"; (2) "the desolateness of the country," which suggested safety; (3) "the probability of some lake" being just beyond; (4) "the malicious judges of my actions" at Jamestown, who might think him lacking in courage; and (5) the desirability of having "some matters of worth to encourage our adventurers [sponsors] in England" (I, 45). The prospective colonists had been told, it will be remembered, to look for such a lake as a likely access to the passage to the Pacific Ocean.

Exploring on foot, accompanied only by an Indian guide, Smith found himself surrounded by 200 men; and, after a fight, he was captured. First brought before the local chieftain, Opeckankenough, Smith was paraded through much of the countryside before finally being delivered to Werawocomoco on the Pamunkey (York) River. There, at the end of December 1607, Smith for the first time saw Powhatan, and what a sight he was!

proudly lying upon a bedstead a foot high upon ten or twelve mats, richly hung with many chains of great pearls about his neck, and covered with a great covering of rahaughcums [raccoon skins]. At his head sat a woman, at his feet another; on each side sitting upon a mat upon the ground were ranged his chief men on each side the fire, ten in a rank, and behind them as many young women, each [with] a great chain of white beads over their shoulders, their heads painted in red, and [Powhatan] with such a grave and majestical countenance as drave me into admiration to see such state in a naked savage. (I, 53)

This description is remarkably vivid despite the omission of some words probably caused by the haste in which Smith was writing—the ship that was to carry his letter to England was ready to weigh anchor—or by the dreadful editing of the letter for publication. Though the work abounds throughout in slips of many kinds, Smith narrates his story well and, as in this passage, with an eye for telling detail and an ability to suggest the personality of the narrator and his reaction to what happened.

In his first interview with Powhatan, which Smith seems to have managed with skill—he knew the importance of picking up a working knowledge of a language in a hurry—he was eager to learn all he could of the new land. Powhatan's extended discourse permitted Smith to reply: "I requited his discourse, seeing what pride he had in his great and spacious dominions, seeing that all he knew were under his territories. In describing to him the territories of Europe which was subject to our great king, whose subject I was,[and] the innumerable multitude of his ships, I gave him to understand the noise of trumpets and terrible manner of fighting [of those that] were under Captain Newport my father, whom I entitled the Meworames, which they call King of All Waters. At his greatness he admired and not a little feared" (I, 56–57). This self-possession in the face of danger is characteristic. It was not merely a literary pose; his colleagues recognized Smith's virtues, unless the fact that he was a self-made man was found to be offensive. In an age not prone to hero worship, Smith's self-portraits may strike readers as pretentious; but one should note that those he left behind remembered him with great admiration when a severe injury forced him to return to England in 1609. The account appears in *The Proceedings*, the narrative portion of *A Map of Virginia* (1612).

What shall I say? but thus we lost him that, in all his proceedings made Justice his first guide and Experience his second, ever hating baseness, sloth, pride, and indignity more than any dangers; that never allowed more for himself than his soldiers with him; that upon no danger would send them where he would not lead them himself; that would never see us want what he either had or could by any means get us; that would rather want than borrow, or starve than not pay; that loved actions more than words and hated falsehood and cozenage worse than death; whose adventures were our lives and whose loss our deaths. (I, 273)

To reject a testimony such as this one takes cynicism, not mere skepticism. Later in his career Smith suffered a series of frustrations and as a consequence indulged in some very unattractive self-pitying; but when he had the opportunity to exercise his capacities, he was a highly successful leader and deserves the title of savior of the Jamestown colony.

Smith's coolheadedness enabled him to make many careful mental notes concerning the land that he saw as a captive and the religious ceremonies of his captors. He later set forth these descriptions with care and precision: the geographical information was of obvious value. He must have thought that the facts about the religious life of the Indians might also prove valuable. Smith's very full picture of the culture of the Indians in his portion of *A Map of Virginia* suggests that he recognized that understanding the Indians' culture was as important as knowing their language in dealing with them.

By the time he was finally returned by the Indians to Jamestown,

Smith had won the friendship of Powhatan: the Indian emperor now sent him supplies once or twice a week. Smith's return did not please some of his jealous colleagues: indeed, only the return of Captain Newport and a supply ship saved Smith's life. He was blamed for the deaths of the two men killed by the Indians when he was captured. Once again Smith enjoyed a hairbreadth escape.

Further Dealings with the Indians

Nearly half of the remainder of A True Relation is devoted to Newport's visit, under Smith's supervision, to Powhatan. Though Smith had good reason to suppose that the Indians were now committed to friendship, he was exceedingly wary. Because he knew "by experience the most of their courages to proceed from others' fear" (I, 63), he made something of a display of his own bravery. First, he made a preliminary visit to Powhatan; then he escorted Newport to the Indian leader. Throughout his narration of this encounter, Smith kept himself in the foreground. It was he who was perpetually on the alert, for he knew that he could believe in Powhatan's friendship only "till convenient opportunity suffered him to betray us" (I, 69). The meetings between the Indians and the English went on for several days during which trading was interspersed with "dancing and much mirth" (I, 75). Finally, the expedition was completed without loss of life, and food for 12 weeks was obtained.

Soon after, on 10 April, Newport returned to England. He left none of the food supplies his ship had brought from England, for his crew had eaten them all. Life at Jamestown settled into a routine not known before. Smith explored the southern end of Chesapeake Bay, then on returning to Jamestown chastened the Indians, who had been stealing tools in abundance. The arrival in late April of a supply ship with new colonists seemed to permit additional exploration, and Smith—above all a military man and always ready for new adventures—and another leader trained a sizable group for six or seven days, apparently including sailors from the ship, to prepare them "to march, fight and skirmish in the woods" (I, 85). When they were ready to start exploring the western reaches beyond the falls of the James River, the plan was vetoed by the ship's captain, who refused to let his men serve without additional pay. Never one to sulk, Smith started the men on tasks at Jamestown, one of which was chopping down trees and preparing lumber for shipment to England; another was planting crops. Smith's official function was still that of supply officer.

The colonists continued to have minor problems with the Indians, who were now plotting to eliminate the English. One plot was revealed when Smith severely frightened a captured Indian into admission of it. In the midst of Smith's not wholly clear account of the Indian–English relations, Powhatan's daughter Pocahontas makes her first appearance in *A True Relation*. Her father had sent her, his favorite, to demonstrate—or rather to counterfeit—his affection for Smith. She was "a child of ten years old which not only for feature, countenance, and proportion much exceedeth any of the rest of his people, but for wit and spirit [is] the only nonpareil of his country" (I, 93). (The phrase was to become a favorite with Smith.) We hear no more of Pocahontas in *A True Relation*.

Smith's methods of dealing with the Indians were extreme, but they had the effect of establishing peace, albeit an uneasy one. Thus, when an Indian saw that his plan to lead Smith and a group of his men into an ambush was not succeeding, Smith "gave him twenty lashes with a rope, and his bow and arrows, bidding him shoot if he durst, and so let him go" (I, 95). With less severe policies later, one consequence was a massacre of the settlers, or so Smith was to reason.

Smith's Outlook

Smith ended *A True Relation* on the state of affairs at the end of May 1608 on a thoroughly optimistic note. Crops had been planted; there was no shortage of food. The colonists had even been able to ship a load of cedar wood to England on the vessel that carried Smith's letter. Smith concluded with a rhetorical flourish: "We now remaining being in good health, all our men well contented, free from mutinies, in love one with another; and as we hope in a continual peace with the Indians, where we doubt not, but by God's gracious assistance and the adventurers' willing minds and speedy furtherance to so honorable an action in after times to see our nation to enjoy a country not only exceeding pleasant for habitation but also very profitable for commerce in general, no doubt pleasing to almighty God, honorable to our gracious sovereign, and commodious generally to the whole kingdom" (I, 97). After the unpleasant report that Smith provided, this conclusion may seem out of place; Philip Barbour notes that "I. H. was primarily responsible for its propagandistic tone" (I, 108, n. 242). But because Smith was consistently optimistic about the possibilities of the New World, perhaps he would have wanted his letter when published to have such an ending. From his point of view, most of the troubles that the colonists had experienced were due to mistakes, inadequate leadership and supplies, and unwillingness to work hard.

Critics of Smith have pointed to his treatment of the leaders of the colony as an example of the bias that they feel vitiates his writings. Smith was highly critical of Captain Edward Maria Wingfield, the first governor, though he wrote little about him. He describes his "audacious command," the lack of harmony on the governing council under Wingfield, and his deposition from the presidency in September 1607 when he "was generally hated of all" for the way that he had conducted the colony's affairs (I, 33, 35). Smith mentions other problems of leadership, but on the whole he was not concerned with the administration of the colony as much as with what was happening. It should not be surprising that his account lacks objectivity, for Smith had a definite point of view—that of a soldier educated chiefly by experience, one who was very much a participant in the affairs of the colony.

A *True Relation* and American Literature

The first American book in English is a lively, detailed, personal account of the first permanent English settlement in America. Moses Coit Tyler rightly observed that Smith "wrote a book that is not unworthy to be the beginning of the new English literature in America."[4] It is valuable not only as a historic document and a landmark in American history but as a work of literature. Its author was a perceptive man as well as a vigorous one. His work has no real structure, for it was written under pressure; but it is not lacking in organization. Instead of composing a chronicle, as many travelers and explorers did, Smith organized much of his material into large blocks, notably those on his capture by the Indians and his visit to Powhatan with Captain Newport. Certain themes tie the work together: the constant danger of attack by the Indians, the lack of knowledge of the area (Chesapeake Bay was largely unexplored, and the falls of the James River had prevented much exploration inland), and the increasing importance of Captain John Smith, the outstanding leader of the colony.

Howard Mumford Jones's study of letters and other writings by early Virginia colonists turned up literate prose in surprising quantity, though not many formal literary productions. From his study, he was led to conclude that Captain John Smith was not "a sport plant in an unliterary wilderness." Common characteristics were shared by this literature, according to Jones; and some of these prove to be characteristic of Smith, not only of his earliest work but of all his literary productions. "For this literature," Jones wrote, "the visible world exists. Its writers see and touch and taste and smell. . . . The vast American landscape has laid its spell upon them. . . ." Among the other qualities of this literature noted by Jones are pragmatism, worldliness, unconcern with theology; in sum, it was a "secular literature."[5] The validity of some of Jones's generalizations for Smith's later writings is limited, for Smith did occasionally become introspective and did sometimes indulge in philosophic and moral meditation. But *A True Relation* is otherwise: it is a thoroughly characteristic piece of seventeenth-century Virginia literature.

By far the fullest and most perceptive treatment of *A True Relation* is that of William Spengemann. He notes that as the work progresses, Smith devotes increasing attention to himself and that this focus is based on Smith's developing relationship with the Indians, some of whose words he carefully introduces into his discourse. "Insofar as Smith's rhetorical self emerges in the course of his narrative progress upriver and expands spatially by way of descriptive digressions into the flanking region discovered there, the self owes its identity largely to the Indians whose lands these are."[6] Smith's "narrative depicts the Virginian interior as coming into being with his discovery of it, as extending only to the limits of his awareness at any moment . . ." (40). This presentation of America and of the self that presents it is for Spengemann characteristically American. "No mind informed by the language of Henry James, Gertrude Stein, and Wallace Stevens will find anything untoward in Smith's tacit identification of history with the career of a single, eventful life or in the propensity of his words to become actions in their own right, rather than a report of completed non-verbal actions" (41). Spengemann's is a strong case for the importance of the book and for Smith's place in American literary history.

Back in England

In October 1609, John Smith was obliged to return to England, after nearly two and a half years in Virginia. He had been badly wounded by a gunpowder explosion, and his year's term as president had expired. He left Virginia with his worst enemies in power. The man appointed to succeed Smith, Sir Thomas Gates, had been shipwrecked in the Bermudas; but the other ships in Gates's fleet had reached Virginia, delivering Captains Gabriel Archer and John Ratcliffe. Both had served with Smith

earlier, and there was no love lost among them. These two, with other
malcontents, prepared an indictment of Smith; he was to answer charges
on his return to London. But there the charges seem to have been largely
dropped. Because Gates had been detained by the shipwreck, Smith
could not know that the Virginia Company's new orders, which appointed Gates governor, named Smith as second member of the Governor's Council and defense chief, an appointment demonstrating the
confidence the company had in Smith.

Without Smith's leadership, the colonists at Jamestown had a difficult time. During the winter following his departure, the "starving
time," scarcely 60 of the augmented colony of 500 survived. Archer and
Ratcliffe were among those who died. In the spring the colony was
abandoned by Gates, who finally had arrived; but before the colonists
could leave Chesapeake Bay, the arrival of a new governor, Lord de la
Warr, stopped the exodus.

In the meanwhile, the Virginia Company had sought to counteract the
rumors current in London concerning the colonists' misadventures. The
company published *A True and sincere declaration of the purposes and ends of
the Plantation begun in Virginia* (London, 1610); but this publication was
not based on any real understanding of what had happened. When even
worse reports reached London, the company published later the same
year a revised version of *A True and sincere declaration*, "with a confutation
of such scandalous reports as have tended to the disgrace of so worthy an
enterprise." This work was an effort to defend the colony's failures with
excuses, some of them untrue. Smith knew the true story from his
experiences, from what returning colonists had reported, and from the
accounts sent back from Virginia. He and some of the other returned
colonists were eager for the truth to be known. With some difficulty they
got their story published, after a clergyman named William Symonds
had edited it into shape. Symonds, who preached in Southwark, near
London, was an Oxford man; perhaps for this reason and because the
London booksellers did not want to offend the Virginia Company, whose
accounts were to be corrected by Symonds's book, *A Map of Virginia* was
published at Oxford, in 1612.

"Description of Virginia"

A Map of Virginia is in two parts. Smith contributed the first part, 39
pages of "a Description of the Country, the Commodities, People,
Government, and Religion, Written by Captaine Smith, sometimes

Governour of the Countrey." (The running title is "The voyages and discoveries of Captaine John Smith of Virginia.") Though he is not named as an author of the second part, *The Proceedings of the English Colonie In Virginia*, Smith had a hand in it, a valuable account that has a separate title page. Smith republished this account with a good many additions and changes as the third book of the *Generall Historie*.

In addition to these two parts, which constitute 149 quarto pages, the book includes a map of Virginia, engraved by William Hole according to Smith's directions. The copper plate prepared by Hole was used again and again—in all, 10 times, with additions being made each time, through 1632. The map was published separately, and it also accompanied the *Generall Historie*. It includes pictorial inserts, most of them based on de Bry's engravings of John White's drawings, which were prepared to accompany the 1590 edition of Thomas Hariot's *A brief and true report*. One pictures Powhatan as he appeared when Smith was his captive in 1607. The map, a very accurate one, is especially valuable because it is "practically the only record of the location of the Indian tribes of Virginia in the early seventeenth century," as Ben McCary observed.[7]

This map and Smith's description are both enlargements of an earlier map and a description ("a relation of the countries and nations that inhabit Virginia") sent by Smith from Virginia in 1608; but neither is extant in its original form. The published map and description are among the most valuable of Smith's legacies, though not primarily as literature. This is not to say that the "Description" is not well-written. As H. M. Jones says, "in both style and organization it shows how excellent an observer Smith could be, how trenchantly he wrote"(48).

The "Description" is perhaps Smith's most permanently interesting work. His biographers have told the story of his life well, and the story of the early days of the Virginia colony is more fully told in modern histories (though, of course, they lack Smith's sense of immediacy); Smith's works on New England seem somewhat dated because of their propagandistic approach, which many readers find unattractive. But the "Description" of Virginia is so consistently entertaining that it is surprising that it has never been republished as a separate work.

Smith's career and training were ideal preparations for the composition of this book. He was very different from those he disparages in the concluding pages, who were "for [the] most part of . . . tender educations and small experience in martial accidents" (I, 176).[8] He knew other lands and other cultures; he could keep his wits in the midst of great danger; he had seen more of Virginia than had any other European; and he had known the Indians as a trader, fighter, and captive. Moreover, he had a good model in Thomas Hariot's book *A brief and true report of the new found land of Virginia* (1588), which had been reprinted in Hakluyt's *Principall Navigations* (1600).

Before *A Map of Virginia* was published, Smith gave his friend Samuel Purchas a manuscript description of Virginia to use in the preparation of the first edition of *Purchas His Pilgrimage*. Though this work did not appear until 1613, the year following the publication of *A Map of Virginia*, Purchas's big book seems to have been in press earlier. Probably Purchas used what Smith gave William Symonds to edit into publishable form. He called it on page 635 "Cap. Smith, M. S." (In the 1625 *Pilgrimes*, Purchas clearly used the published book, not the manuscript of the *Pilgrimage* version; he reprinted the whole of the "Description.") The *Pilgrimage* version may provide a good idea of what Smith wrote for Symonds, though it may have been revised somewhat by Purchas himself. These parallel passages are from the two printed versions:

Purchas, *Purchas His Pilgrimage*	*A Map of Virginia*
The chief god they worship is the devil, which they call *Oke*.	But their chief god they worship is the devil. Him they call *Oke* and serve him more of fear than love.
They have conference with him, and fashion themselves unto his shape.	They say they have conference with him, and fashion themselves as near to his shape as they can imagine.
In their temples they have his image ill-favoredly made,	In their temples they have his image evil-favoredly carved and then
painted, adorned with chains, copper, and beads, and covered with a skin,	painted and adorned with chains, copper, and beads, and covered with a skin, in such manner as the deformity may well suit with such a god.
By him is commonly the sepulcher of their kings, whose bodies are first	By him is commonly the sepulcher of their kings. Their bodies are first

boweled, then dried on a hurdle,	boweled, then dried upon hurdles till they be very dry, and so about the
and have about the joints	most of their joints and neck they
chains of coppers, beads, and other like	hang bracelets or chains of copper, pearl, and such like, as they use to wear; their inwards they stuff with copper beads and cover with a skin,
trash; Then lapped in white skins, and rolled in mats,	hatchets, and such trash. Then lap they them very carefully in white skins, and so roll them in mats,
and entombed in arches made of mats,	for their winding sheets. And in the tomb, which is an arch made of mats, they lay them
the remnant	orderly. What remaineth of this kind
of their wealth being set	of wealth their kings have, they set
at their feet.	at their feet in baskets.
These temples and bodies are kept by their	These temples and bodies are kept by their
priests. (639)	priests. (I, 169)

The version in *A Map of Virginia* is full of editorializing such as one might expect of a Christian clergyman. The *Pilgrimage* version is more condensed. Purchas's version is probably closer to what Smith wrote, though Purchas may have trimmed what Smith gave him, as he seems to have done with Smith's autobiography (see chapter 7).

Smith begins the work with a vocabulary of Indian words and phrases. Besides the Indian words for numbers and other common expressions, Smith demonstrates the Algonkian language by giving in Algonkian and English such revealing phrases as "Bid Pocahontas bring hither two little baskets, and I will give her white beads to make her a chain," and "Run

you then to the king Mawmarynough and bid him come hither" (I, 139).
As Barbour comments on this passage, the reference to Pocahontas
"shows how he thought of her before her arrival in London in 1616."

Smith as Natural Historian

The "Description" proper begins with geography: the climate, the
shape of the land, the rivers, a catalogue of the inhabitants. This section
is full of interesting observations, some of which reveal an eye sensitive to
beauty: "The country is not mountainous nor yet low but such pleasant
plain hills and fertile valleys, one prettily crossing another, and watered
so conveniently with their sweet brooks and crystal springs as if art itself
had devised them" (I, 145), Smith was especially impressed with the
Susquehannock Indians, who lived at the northern end of Chesapeake
Bay:

Such great and well proportioned men are seldom seen, for they seemed like
giants to the English, yea and to the neighbors, yet seemed of an honest and
simple disposition [and were] with much ado restrained from adoring the
discoverers as gods. Those are the most strange people of all those countries,
both in language and attire. For their language it may well beseem their
proportions, sounding from them as it were a great voice in a vault or cave, as an
echo. Their attire is the skins of bears and wolves. Some have cassocks made of
bears' heads and skins that a man's neck goes through the skin's neck and the
ears of the bear fastened to his shoulders behind, the nose and teeth hanging
down his breast, and at the end of the nose hung a bear's paw. (I, 149)

The next sections of the "Description," which resemble Hariot's *A
brief and true report*, deal with the usual plants growing naturally and in
cultivated fashion, and the products that Virginia could produce for
export. This last section is Smith's extended propaganda plea for America, the sort of thing that became his chief concern when he was not able
to return to either Virginia or New England. He argued that Virginia
could produce the same commodities that were bringing wealth to
England's competitors: Muscovy, Poland, Sweden, France, Spain, Italy,
and Holland. Virginian products were within 100 miles "to be had,
either ready provided by nature or else to be prepared, were there but
industrious men to labor" (I, 159).

Despite the unrestrained optimism of this passage and a few others,
the tone of most of the work is cautious; Smith's motive was "to satisfy

my friends of the true worth and quality of Virginia" (I, 175). He had little use for those who wanted quick and easy wealth, particularly that obtained from gold. He reported little certain information on mineral resources since skilled refiners had not been available. He scoffed at those who found "shining stones and spangles" and flattered themselves "in their own vain conceits to have been supposed what they were not" (I, 156).

More than his optimism or his practicality, what impresses one most about Smith's account is his extensive knowledge. Sometimes it is revealed in minor observations, as when he noted that Indian peas resemble what the Italians call *fagioli* and that Indian beans resemble what the Turks call *garnanses*. But chiefly one is impressed by Smith's knowledge of natural phenomena: Indian medicines and herbs, seventeen varieties of animals, including bears "very little in comparison of those of Muscovia and Tartaria" (I, 155), and 20 kinds of fish.

Smith on the Virginia Indians

Smith devoted the second half of his "Description" to the Indians: their appearance, way of life, hunting and fishing, warfare, medicine, religion, and government. As Jones has observed, Smith did not always comprehend what he saw, "But his devouring eye has missed nothing" (49). Since he made his observations, as he himself noted, mainly as a prisoner of the Indians (I, 165), the acuteness of his report is all the more remarkable.

Keith Glenn's essay, "Captain John Smith and the Indians," attempts to provide a historical context for Smith's attitude toward the Indians. She observes that some Englishmen considered it unlawful to colonize lands occupied by other peoples, especially because cruel and oppressive treatment of the natives were a likely result, as Spanish practices had shown: much was therefore made of the missionary value of colonization as a justification of it. This view implied a kind of equality between white men and Indians. The Virginia Company had specifically instructed the colonists: ". . . you must have great care not to offend the naturals, if you can eschew it." In Glenn's view, Smith considered that the London instructions were intended to be a means to an end—the establishment of a successful colony—and that the Indians were in fact obstacles to the achievement of this objective, and therefore he adopted an attitude very different from the official one. Glenn argues that Smith believed that the Indians should be subjugated and, once put in their place, made to work for the colonists in such tasks as they could best perform: growing corn, hunting, and fishing. It might be added that Smith considered the Indians useful as guides on how to survive in the American wilderness. This policy of subjugation was offensive to the Virginia Company of London until Indian massacres of the English made it seem wiser.[9] In the "Description" he sought, in part, to be a reporter on the Indians because to know their ways would permit one to learn from them.

Roy Harvey Pearce has noted that Smith believed that the Indians occupied "the naturally minimal order of savage life, with its natural aspiration towards the higher life of Christian civility."[10] This assumption was, of course, common among the English of Smith's time. It is, however, hardly fair to write, as did Pearce, that Smith saw the Indians as mere savages. He did indeed write that "some are of disposition fearful, some bold, most cautelous [deceitful, tricky], all savage" (I, 160). But clearly he was more impressed with their abilities, as craftsmen, as woodsmen, and as warriors. (Smith was always the soldier.) "They are very strong, of an able body and full of agility, able to endure to lie in the woods under a tree by the fire in the worst of winter, or in the weeds and grass, in ambuscado in the summer" (I, 160). He looked at their skill in warfare like an old soldier: in the attack there is "on each flank a sergeant, and in the rear an officer for lieutenant, all duly keeping their orders, yet leaping and singing after their accustomed tune, which they use only in wars" (I, 167).

One of the weaknesses of those who have written about Smith's attitudes toward the Indians is that they failed to recognize that, like most other English observers, he distinguished between low-born and high-born Indians. Smith's criticism of Indians is analogous to his criticism of his fellow Englishmen. Among both he found people who were treacherous. Even though Smith had managed to be upwardly mobile, he was profoundly aware of class distinctions. As Karen Kupperman observes, marks of barbarism were noted by English observers such as Smith among both Indians and the "civilized" Englishmen.[11] Smith could not be expected to escape his cultural values, as a modern anthropologist seeks to do, contrary to J. A. Leo Lemay's assertion that "Smith judged the degree of civility among Indians according to religion, weapons, agriculture, vocabulary, and government—among other standards—but he never thought they were inferior. Like the different nations of Europe, they were at different stages of socioeconomic, religious, and cultural development."[12]

Smith notes with some disgust that "the common sort have scarce to cover their nakedness but with grass, the leaves of trees, or such like"; he describes with satisfaction a mantle of turkey feathers "so prettily wrought and woven with threads that nothing could be discerned but the feathers" (I, 161). Smith does not emphasize the inferiority of the Indians; on the contrary, many of his comparisons stress their abilities. Thus, he notes that they do not use oars but instead "use paddles and sticks, with which they will row faster than our barges" (I, 163). But it was the Indians' adaptability that Smith especially admired: they "know all the advantages and places most frequented with deer, beasts, fish, fowl, roots, and berries" (I, 164).

Smith was an optimistic, practical, careful observer, working of course from the assumptions of his time but showing real interest in and rarely condescension toward the Indians. He was surprisingly objective, if tough-minded. Thus, Smith reports without comment that in large holes made in their ears some Indians wear "a small green-and-yellow-colored snake, near half a yard in length, which, crawling and lapping herself about his neck, oftentimes familiarly would kiss his lips" (I, 161). Indians treat a guest generously, Smith reports, again without comment: "at night, where his lodging is appointed, they set a woman fresh painted red with pacones and oil, to be his bedfellow" (I, 168). Whether Smith received this generous treatment is not reported. In his comments on Indian religion Smith is perhaps least perceptive, but his account is interesting, comprehensive, full of detail. His reactions to Indian religion occasionally reflect his values (he had definite religious convictions), as when he noted, "Before their dinners and suppers, the better sort will take the first bit and cast it in the fire, which is all the grace they are known to use" (I, 171).

Perry Miller has demonstrated that, according to the early literature of Virginia, a prime motive in the establishment of the colony was the conversion of the Indians to Christianity.[13] Smith had little to say about this goal. He does indeed characterize Virginia as "a nurse for soldiers, a practice for mariners, a trade for merchants, a reward for the good, and that which is most of all, a business (most acceptable to God) to bring such poor infidels to the true knowledge of God and His Holy Gospel" (I, 159). But his observations on the Indians do not suggest that the statement be taken with much seriousness. Though he was appalled by the Indians' worship of the ugly, evil idol Oke, and though he lamented their ignorance of their true creator, he was all too aware that the best endeavors of the English "to divert them from this blind idolatry" got them nowhere (I, 172), for the Indians merely considered that their gods were inferior to the stronger ones of the English.

The most unsatisfactory aspect of Smith's treatment of the Indians is his report of an annual "sacrifice of children." Smith describes as much as he (or another Englishman) saw; but important parts of the ceremony, he noted, were "not seen" (I, 172). Ben McCary identified the ceremony with the Huskanaw, which was a kind of initiation or hardening and testing.[14] Philip Barbour describes it as a puberty rite and suggests that the children were not sacrificed but kept for a time from their mothers.[15]

In the last section on Indian government, Smith again emphasizes the capacities of the Indians, not their inferiority: "their magistrates for good commanding and their people for due subjection and obeying excel many places that would be counted very civil" (I, 173). Most of the chapter is devoted to Powhatan, the Indian emperor—his jurisdiction, dealings with the inferior kings or werowances, treasury, justice, system of punishments. Among the punishments is one with which Smith nearly had personal experience, according to the account in *Generall Historie*: "Sometimes he causeth the heads of them that offend him to be laid upon the altar or sacrificing stone, and one with clubs beats out their brains" (I, 174–175). If Smith barely escaped this form of execution, it is not surprising that he next cited the excruciating means used to kill George Cusson, who had been a member of Smith's party when he was captured: Powhatan "causeth him to be tied to a tree, and with mussel shells or reeds, the executioner cutteth off his joints one after another, ever casting what they cut off into the fire. Then doth he proceed with shells and reeds to case the skin from his head and face. Then do they rip his belly and so burn him with the tree and all" (I, 175).

Setting the Record Straight

The last pages of the "Description" demonstrate once again that *A Map of Virginia* was written to set the record straight. Here Smith attacks in blunt fashion those colonists who pretended to be experts on things Virginian "though they were scarce ever ten miles from Jamestown" (I, 175). These same, he protests, were themselves a "plague to us in Virginia." Nevertheless, all went well "so long after as I did govern there, until I left the country" (I, 176, 177).

With this personal note, Smith ends the work. A proud man, Smith chose not to write an extended defense of himself, though he expresses satisfaction that the second part of *A Map of Virginia* provides a full report. Indeed, it is a vindication of Smith; and, lest he should appear thin-skinned, it should be noted that two of the authors of the second part report "foul slanders" of Smith, "urged for truths by many a hundred that do still not spare to spread them, say them, and swear them" (I, 275). But, instead of writing a personal testament, Smith wrote a precise account of the Virginia he knew so well; packed with information, objective yet far from cold, detailed but not dull, his is the work of an immensely perceptive man whose bold adventures led him to know what a less active man never could have discovered. Richard Beale Davis notes that in his second work, "the fiber of the man shows through the Jacobean corselet, a 'new gentleman' risen from the yeomanry, a leader who believed that character, common sense, and perceptivity were the only means of building a new nation among Stone Age savages in a land of natural abundance."[16]

The "Description" is highly valued by ethnologists and anthropologists. With the broader view of history that has been adopted in the twentieth century, Smith's brief study should be recognized as of great historical importance. Because Smith's later original contributions to the *Generall Historie* in Book III are fragmentary and less objective, the "Description" is really Smith's most important contribution to historical studies.

The Proceedings

Following *A Map of Virginia* in the same volume but with a separate title page is *The Proceedings of the English Colonie In Virginia since their first beginning from England in the yeare of our Lord 1606, till this present 1612.* The title page proceeds to explain that the work is *out of the writings of Thomas Studley the first provant maister, Anas Todkill, Walter Russell Doctor of Phisicke, Nathaniell Powell, William Phettplace, Richard Wyffin, Thomas Abbay, Tho: Hope, Rich: Potts and the labours of divers other diligent observers, that were residents in Virginia. And perused and confirmed by diverse now resident in England that were actors in this busines.* Finally the editor, if that is the term, is identified: *By W. S.* This work resulted from an effort to provide a comprehensive account of the early years of the colony. "W. S." has been identified as the Rev. William Symonds. Barbour assigned the first two chapters to Smith though the name printed at the end of chapter 2 is Thomas Studley, who had died in 1607. The first chapter records the organization of the Virginia venture, briefly describes the voyage and arrival in Virginia, and offers a succinct account of the events taking place before the departure of Captain Christopher Newport on 15 June 1607. The second chapter is written in a far more personal style and reads very much like Smith's other writings. It deals with events after June and before the arrival of the first supply ships at the beginning of 1609. (All dates are new style.)

Much of the chapter focuses on food shortages and problems of leadership, with Smith gradually being recognized as the only suitable leader. He was even obliged to prevent the other leaders from abandoning the colony. In time, "the winter approaching, the rivers became so covered with swans, geese, ducks, and cranes that we daily feasted. . . ." "But our comedies never endured long without a tragedy; some idle exceptions [were] being muttered against Captain Smith for not discovering the head of the Chickahominy River and [he was] taxed by the [Governing] Council to be too slow in so worthy an attempt" (I, 212). Smith then attempted to go up that river, but he and his party were captured by the Indians whose leader was Powhatan and remained as their prisoners for a month. According to the account in the *Generall Historie*, it was at this time that Smith was rescued from death by Pocahontas. In the account in *The Proceedings*, nothing is said of Pocahontas, merely that Smith "so demeaned himself amongst them [the Indians] as he not only diverted them from surprising the fort but procured his own liberty and got himself and his company [his fellow English captives] such estimation amongst them that those savages admired him as a demi-god" (I, 213).

The writers of the remainder of *The Proceedings* presumably relied on Smith, either his words or his memory, from time to time, as when speeches that Smith delivered to the colonists or to the Indians are quoted.[17] But the student of Smith's writings cannot be confident that what he is reading is what Smith wrote. Especially to be noted is what editor William Symonds wrote in an afterword: "Captain Smith, I return you the fruits of my labors. . . . The pains I took was great . . ." (I, 278). Because Smith revised and amplified all of these pages of *The Proceedings* when he came to compile the *Generall Historie*, I judge it best to refrain from further discussion of the 1612 work here. The additions to it, discussed in chapter 5, are clearly Smith's.

Chapter Four

The Compiler: *The Generall Historie*

Captain John Smith's most famous work is *The Generall Historie of Virginia, New-England, and the Summer Isles*. It has been judged worthy to rank with the histories of William Bradford, Edward Johnson, and John Winthrop; indeed, Smith has been called "the father of Anglo–American History."[1] The *Generall Historie* is complex, uneven, and controversial. According to one commentator, "John Smith's *General Historie* is an important part of the deeper cultural consciousness" that has sustained the "perennial faith in the promise of American life." The heart of the *Generall Historie*, Books III and IV, is said to "have a dramatic rhythm and an exciting vividness that charmed Americans for generations."[2] The *Generall Historie* is an important but much misunderstood book. Smith's role was at least as much that of compiler as of author.

Circumstances of Composition

The origin of the *Generall Historie* appears to have been an occasion in April 1621, when John Smythe of Nibley, a Gloucestershire man who had invested in the Virginia Company of London, stated at a meeting of the company that the Virginia colony would benefit from "a fair and perspicuous history, compiled of that country, from her discovery to this day." He moved publication of such a "general history," as he called it, that would serve as a memorial of the colony and preserve for posterity truth that might otherwise suffer the ravages of time—or so thought John Smythe.[3] His motion was commended by those attending the meeting, but no action was taken. At the time, the colony was in good health; it seemed at last to be thriving. But in March 1622, the Indians of Virginia rose and killed about 400 colonists. Captain John Smith soon requested the Virginia Company to send him, with 100 soldiers and 30 sailors, "to enforce the savages to leave their country, or bring them in that fear and subjection that every man should follow their business securely."[4] The Company expressed little intelligent interest in Smith's plan, however, and Smith was again frustrated. The Indian attack did have one important consequence: the Virginia Company was dissolved by action of the Court of King's Bench. It was during the period 1623–24, when the future of Virginia was uncertain, that Smith wrote his history, no doubt out of disappointment. Perhaps he hoped that a reorganized company of backers would find a place for him. At any rate he sought to assist the cause of American colonization by writing.

John Smith was a likely man to pick up a proposal for a history of Virginia, for he knew the colony well, cared much for its welfare, wanted his name to be associated with it, and was experienced as a writer. Since he also knew New England, he decided to include it in his history; moreover, he could thereby include his earlier writings on New England. A more skillful writer, William Strachey, had begun *The Historie of Travell into Virginia Britannia* (which for him also included New England); but he had given up the work before his death in 1621. How Smith chose to include the Bermudas is not clear; perhaps he came across appealing documents and decided to use them.

In 1623, Smith prepared much of Book I of the *Generall Historie*; by the end of the year he had prepared and had published a prospectus so detailed as to indicate that the work was well along, and perhaps completed. In this prospectus, included in the Barbour edition, Smith explains, "These observations are all I have for the expenses of a thousand pound, and the loss of eighteen years of time, besides all the travels, dangers, miseries, and encumbrances for my country's good I have endured gratis" (II, 16). The prospectus was intended to raise funds to support publication; he pleaded he needed nearly £100. How much was raised in this fashion, if any, is not known; but Smith did find a patron in the very wealthy Duchess of Richmond and Lenox, to whom the *Generall Historie* is dedicated, and without whose bounty, Smith writes in a dedication, "it had died in the womb." In a striking passage Smith explains, "That which hath been endured and passed through with hardship and danger is thereby sweetened to the Actor when he becometh the Relator. I have deeply hazarded myself in doing and suffering, and why should I stick to hazard my reputation in recording? He that acteth two parts is the more born withal if he come short or fail in one of them" (II, 41, 42). Of this passage and more largely of Smith's presentation of himself in the *Generall Historie*, Lewis Simpson has acutely noted:

Instead of emulating the actor as bard by responding to a firmly established concept of the actor-relator defined by his community, Smith is closer to assuming the modern character of the actor-relator, a mutant creature who appears only when the technological achievement of printing begins to become definitive in Western culture. As the author of a printed book—a manufactured object, available in multiple copies, made to be held in many hands yet in the hands of only one person—Smith expresses the relationship between author and reader as a part of the experience of individuation accompanying the development of secular history as the mode of existence. This experience is particularly intense for the author; his book, an embodiment of himself brought forth into time, lives only in the favoring response of the reader. The writer images a close familiarity—a sweetness of association—with an audience, which, whether composed of one person or many, is not merely his patron but the necessity of his being.[5]

The completed book was published in 1624, a handsome folio volume of 241 pages with an attractive engraved title page; four engraved maps (Ould Virginia or the Roanoke colony area, Virginia, the Summer Isles [the Bermudas], and New England); some copies even had portraits of Pocahontas and the Duchess of Richmond and Lenox. Both an ordinary and a large paper edition were published. Two printers prepared the work, and by a miscalculation there are no pages numbered 95–104, though there is no gap in the text itself. Six later editions or issues of the *Generall Historie* were published between 1626 and 1632, but these prove to have been unsold copies of the original printing, with new title pages and some changes in the map. It is appropriate that the Barbour edition is unusually handsome, for in its original form the *Generall Historie* is much embellished; besides the maps and portraits, it is decorated with a flowery dedication and a good deal of verse: 10 complimentary poems, including one by Smith's friend Samuel Purchas. Also throughout the text bits of more or less appropriate verse appear, largely translations of classical authors, borrowed with a few changes from Bishop Martin Fotherby's *Atheomastix* (1622). Smith seems to have picked up the idea of using poetry in this fashion from George Sandys's *Relation of a Journey*, published in 1615.[6]

It is important to note that Smith set out to make the *Generall Historie* a collection such as those made by Richard Hakluyt and Samuel Purchas, especially Purchas, who assisted him with the book. Like Purchas, Smith was not so much historian as compiler. Smith's most substantial contribution appears in Book III, in which appear almost 10,000 words of new material (see chapter 6).

The first four books of the *Generall Historie* deal mainly with Virginia. Book I provides a history of the Roanoke colony and early visits to New England; Book II describes the land and people of the Jamestown area; and Books III and IV relate the history of the Virginia colony through 1624. Book V deals with the Bermudas, and Book VI reports the history of New England beginning with Smith's visit in 1614. In *The True Travels* (1630), Smith continues and extends the *Generall Historie*, with brief reports on English colonial efforts in Guiana and the West Indies.

The *Generall Historie* begins with a brief preface "of four points." Three cite the virtues of having colonies: they bring honor to the King by spreading Christianity and enriching the English monarchy; they serve as an excellent investment; and they provide an opportunity for the industrious and virtuous to get ahead. In his last point, Smith states his method of handling his sources: ". . . now my care hath been that my relations should give every man they concern, their due. But had I not discovered and lived in the most of those parts, I could not possibly have collected the substantial truth from such a number of variable relations, that would make a volume at least of a thousand sheets" (II, 44). One thousand sheets would be 4,000 folio pages.

Book One

Without further explanation—and some additions would have been helpful—the work begins. Seven paragraphs tell, in extremely condensed form, of the mythological and historical discovery of America, English explorations under the Cabots, and the work of Frobisher and Gilbert. The first block of material follows: a report on the first voyage of 1584 made to America under Sir Walter Raleigh. Smith's source is an account in Richard Hakluyt's *Principal Navigations* written by Arthur Barlow, one of two ship captains who led the expedition.[7] At first Smith shifts from the first person of his source to the third person, but in the second paragraph he picks up Barlow's point of view. Smith summarizes and at times rearranges the order of what Barlow had written, an indication that he took some time to prepare his work. At one point he notes that he was using "the author's own phrase"; in fact, nearly everything is in the phrasing of Smith's author. At another point Smith uses the expression "the author sayth," perhaps because he was doubtful that the statement supplied was correct. In about half as many words as the original, Smith told the interesting and important story of the voyage.

For his next account Smith uses the next one in Hakluyt's *Principal Navigations*. This time the source is a log of another voyage to Roanoke, severely condensed. Then he employs another document from Hakluyt, an account by the governor of the colony, Ralph Lane.

Smith's next source, Thomas Hariot's *A brief and true report*, was reprinted—in condensed form—in Hakluyt, and from that condensation Smith drew his material. He reprints only a little material from Hariot, however, presumably because in Book II Smith's own "Description" of Virginia covers much of the same subject. Thus he notes that the North Carolina Indians' "clothing, towns, houses, wars, arts, tools, handicrafts, and educations, are much like them in that part of Virginia we now inhabit; which at large you may read in the description thereof. But the relation of their religion is strange, as this author reporteth" (II, 78). Then follows an account of the North Carolina Indians' religion.

Smith continues to follow Hakluyt all the way to the end of the account on Roanoke. Then with only a part of an original sentence for transition he begins to borrow again. "All hopes of Virginia thus abandoned, it lay dead and obscured from 1590 till this year 1602, that Captain Gosnold, with thirty-two and himself in a small bark, set sail from Dartmouth upon the twenty-sixth of March" (II, 88). Smith's borrowing is then from John Brereton's *Brief and True Relation* (London, 1602), which tells of a voyage to Cape Cod. Smith revises distances and dates, condenses Brereton's effective descriptions (quoted in chapter 1), and weakens an interesting report; this part is, therefore, much less attractive than it might have been.

Though most readers of Book I are aware that little of Smith's material is original, just how closely Smith followed his sources is not so evident. Here is how he revised a portion of Brereton's account:

Brereton	*Smith*
But not to cloy you with particular rehearsal of such things as God and Nature hath bestowed on these places, in comparison whereof, the most fertile part of all England is (of itself) but barren. (7)	. . . but not to cloy you with particulars, what God and nature hath bestowed on those places, I refer you to the author's own writing at large. (II, 90)

Smith was enthusiastic about New England, but he was determined to be cautious in his commendations.

For the remaining two portions of Book I, on voyages to New England, Smith used two reports that Samuel Purchas was to publish in 1625.[8] The second is James Rosier's *True Relation* (1605), for which Smith seems to have used the abridged version—he may have used printer's proofs—that was to appear in *Purchas His Pilgrimes*.[9]

Book I of Smith's *Generall Historie* is a comprehensive account of pre–Jamestown English exploration in America. It was easily compiled, for Smith had only to consult Hakluyt's great *Navigations*, his friend Purchas's collection of documents, and probably an additional published account, Brereton's. Everything in Book I is available elsewhere in fuller form, but it serves as an appropriate prologue to the rest of the *Generall Historie*.

Book Two

Entitled "The Sixth Voyage. 1606. To another part of Virginia," Book II is a reprint of Smith's own "Description" of Virginia. Smith made no attempt to justify its inclusion: it is simply another document relating to Virginia, and he made very few revisions. He shifted the narrative portions from the third to the first person, presumably to make the book correspond to other narratives; and he made a very few deletions and additions. He notes, for example, that an Indian ceremony he had described in *A Map of Virginia* was more properly characterized later as part of the narrative of his captivity in Book III; he moved and enlarged it. To his expression of regret that the Indians were ignorant of true religion, he adds in the *Generall Historie*, "and we had not language sufficient so plainly to express it as make them understand it, which God grant they may" (II, 125).

Smith sought to impose on his materials no unity of any kind. He aimed merely to eliminate from the sources he had collected whatever "would tire any wise man" (II, 474): patents, treaties, directions and the like. Some portions of the *Generall Historie* do hang together because of the vague sense of Smith's personality that shows through the writing, but very little of this quality is found in Book I, where Smith's task was simply that of digester of other men's writings, or even in Book II, where, although the whole is Smith's writing, the tone is the least personal of his original works. Nevertheless, the last words of the book are these: "John Smith writ this with his own hand" (II, 129).

Book Three

Book III, of which Smith wrote nearly one-fourth especially for the *Generall Historie*, is quite different. Because Smith's reputation as a historian rests mostly on this book, it is best discussed in Chapter 6. It suffices to say here that it is a coherent account of the events that took place in Virginia from 1607 to 1609, based on *The Proceedings*, the report prepared by Smith's friends and published in 1612 as part of *A Map of Virginia*. Smith was fortunate to have such a substantial and lively basis for the book, of which his own contribution was the liveliest, whether he is considered subject or author.

Book Four

Book IV is of almost equal importance to students of Smith's writings and very important for a consideration of his work as a compiler. It tells the story of Virginia after Smith's departure. From what his supporters had written about the conduct of the colony by those who succeeded him in its government, it might be expected that Smith would indulge in some special pleading, but one is scarcely prepared for what is found. Even admirers of Smith would find it difficult to praise this collection of miscellaneous documents.[10]

After a clear and coherent beginning, Smith includes in almost random fashion whatever he could locate related to the colony in any way: an announcement of a lottery for Virginia, an extended account of a sea fight in the West Indies (dragged in on the grounds that one of the participating ships was on its way to Virginia), a list of items that each immigrant to Virginia should possess, and a 12–page list of the "adventurers for Virginia . . . according to a printed book." One theme runs through Book IV: Smith was the only real expert on Virginia, and he alone knew what should have been done and what should be done now.

Editorializing of various kinds occupies nearly one-fourth of the book. Smith describes his project for subduing the Indians who had recently massacred the settlers; he includes "a brief relation written by Captain Smith to his Majesty's Commissioners for the reform of Virginia, concerning some aspersions against it," and answers to seven questions that Smith supplied to the commissioners, presumably in 1623. As might be expected, he declared that "Idleness and carelessness brought all I did in three years in six months to nothing" (II, 327). He sensibly recognized that the government of the colony had been mishandled and urged that the King take charge.

At the end of the book Smith attempts to justify his procedure of including all manner of information. Perhaps he did discern the weakness of this portion, but his apology is inadequate because it does not explain why the book is in such large measure devoted to Smith's case for himself: "Thus far I have travelled in this wilderness of Virginia, not being ignorant [that] for all my pains this discourse will be wrested, tossed and turned as many ways as there is leaves; that I have writ too much of some, too little of others, and many such like objections. To such I must answer in the Company's name I was requested to do it. If any have concealed their approved experiences from my knowledge they must excuse me. As for every fatherless or stolen relation, I leave them to the charge of them that desire them" (II, 333). What Smith wrote may be true, though there is no evidence that he was requested by the Virginia Company to prepare the *Generall Historie*; and he made no effort to defend the company but instead was often critical of it. It should be said for Smith that a bibliography of contemporary accounts of Virginia indicates little of significance that Smith might have used but did not.[11] A notable exception, perhaps, is an unpublished account by John Rolfe on the state of the colony in 1616, a period rather neglected in the *Generall Historie*; but Smith may not have known about this narrative. Later historians have of course been able to draw on sources that Smith did not have access to.

Smith reprints in abridged form a good many pages of writings previously published. Among the best-covered years are those reported by two of these documents: Ralph Hamor's *True Discourse of the Present Estate of Virginia* (1615), which deals with the years 1611–14, and Edward Waterhouse's *A Declaration of the state of the colony and affairs in Virginia* (1622), which reports on the massacre of 1622. Smith condensed, rephrased, and revised these works and even on occasion added information to his sources. Thus Hamor's criticism of Jeffrey Abbots aroused Smith to comment: "Here I entreat your patience for an apology though not a pardon. This Jeffrey Abbots, however this author censures him, and the Governor executes him, I know he had long served both in Ireland and Netherlands. Here he was a sergeant of my company, and I never saw in Virginia a more sufficient soldier, less turbulent, a better wit, more hardy or industrious, nor any more forward to cut off them that sought to abandon the country or wrong the colony" (II, 240).

Hamor's account is very detailed, and Smith's digest is an intelligent one. He trims Hamor's propaganda, but on occasion inserts some of his own:

Hamor	*Smith*
Pocahontas (whose fame hath even been spread in England by the title of non parella of Virginia) . . . (4)	Pocahontas, whom Captain Smith's relations entitleth the numparell of Virginia . . . (II, 243)

Book IV does include some private letters not available elsewhere, for example a few pages on Lord de la Warr as Governor by William Box (II, 234–37). But this section is indeed fundamentally Captain John Smith's apologia. He lists for the King's commissioners the great accomplishments of the years when he was present in Virginia: the subjection of the Indians, the shipment of valuable commodities to England (timber, pitch, tar, samples of ore, and the like); the building of Jamestown with 40 or 50 houses and three forts; and the planting of corn:

We had but six ships to transport and supply us, and but 277 men, boys, and women, by whose labors Virginia being brought to this kind of perfection, the most difficulties past, and the foundation thus laid by this small means. Yet because we had done no more, they called in our commission, took a new in their own names, and appointed us near as many offices and officers as I had soldiers, that neither knew us nor we them—without our consents or knowledge. Since, there have gone more than one hundred ships of other proportions, and eight or ten thousand people. Now if you please to compare what hath been spent, sent, discovered, and done this fifteen years by that we did in the three first years, and every governor that hath been there since give you but such an account as this, you may easily find what hath been the cause of those disasters in Virginia. (II, 325)

Not one to hide his talent under a bushel, Smith explains Virginia's problems as the absence of himself.

Similarly, Book IV contains a long digression in which Smith protests that the "first adventurers" had not benefited from the colony as was intended and that many of the most deserving and industrious (the reader would understand that Smith was among them) had profited far less than the nobility and gentry (II, 255–56). Perhaps the subjective tone of these comments is best explained by Smith's statement that he may be "too bold to censure other men's actions" when he himself had not been in Virginia for years, but that others who had never been to Virginia had censured him. Lest his readers suppose that he was merely being vindictive, he declares that his motives were "the glory of God, the honor of my country, and the public good" (II, 303–4).

Much of the history that Book IV surveys demonstrated to Smith the wisdom of his own policies. He points to the lack of continuity in leadership and to the weakness of the governors, especially in dealing with the Indians. The massacre of 1622 was for Smith a complete vindication of his own tough Indian policy, and he repeats his recommendations for dealing with the Indians so frequently that he could write at one point: "The manner how to suppress them is so often related and approved, I omit it here. And you have twenty examples of the Spaniards how they got the West Indies and forced the treacherous and rebellious infidels to do all manner of drudgery work and slavery for them, themselves living like soldiers upon the fruits of their labors. This will make us more circumspect and be an example to posterity. (But I say, this might as well have been put in practice sixteen years ago as now)" (II, 299). This passage is followed by three pages of "Encouragements": Smith urges recognition that failures should lead only to greater efforts.

Smith's optimism frequently saves his editorializing from tediousness. Similarly appealing is his sense of America's limitless possibilities: "Let us with all speed take the priority of time, where also may be had the priority of place, in choosing the best seats of the country, which now by vanquishing the savages, is like to offer a more fair and ample choice of fruitful habitations than hitherto our gentleness and fair comportments could attain unto" (II, 301).

But the editorializing still is objectionable because the accounts comprising Book IV are primarily narratives of adventures, full of encounters with the Indians, and the regular interjections of "Captain Smith's opinion" are an annoying interruption. Furthermore, Smith was probably ignorant of the work of the Virginia Company of London, the routine of whose meetings would have seemed both dull and unimportant to him. J. Franklin Jameson's observation is relevant: Smith "writes, by preference, of encounters, of explorations, of opportunities for present gains, as one who is directing a band of adventurers. . . ."[12] As a result of the emphasis on action (and the editorializing), Smith's history lacks perspective and balance: it contains close-ups but no background is visible, no panoramic views. In Book IV, even Smith's ability to compose an orderly series of pictures collapsed. His frustrations and disappoint-

ments got the best of him, and his carefully edited collection of documents degenerated into a vindication of John Smith.

A final example of how Smith's egotism damaged the plan of the
Generall Historie should suffice. In Book IV, Smith includes his earliest
account of his rescue by Pocahontas—the earliest if the letter that he
published in the *Generall Historie* is indeed "an abstract" of "a little
book" written to Queen Anne to make Pocahontas's virtues known to the
Queen and her court. Smith's excuse for publishing it is merely that it
relates to a Virginia Indian's visit to London in 1616. According to this
account, "After some six [actually four] weeks' fatting amongst those
savage courtiers, at the minute of my execution she hazarded the beating
out of her own brains to save mine, and not only that but so prevailed
with her father that I was safely conducted to Jamestown . . ."
(II, 259). Philip Barbour defends Smith's writing of the letter on the
occasion of Pocahontas's visit to London as "an opportunity to do
something for her and at the same time promote his own interest"
(II, 258 note), but he does not attempt to defend the inclusion of the
letter in the *Generall Historie.* The modern reader will find the letter to be
an attractive sketch of the girl Smith remembered from his Jamestown
days. The Pocahontas letter occupies several pages of Book IV.

Book Five

Book V is different from the other parts of the *Generall Historie* because
Smith never visited the Bermudas, the subject of the book; he therefore
found little occasion for editorializing. The book is mostly a digest of one
source, Nathaniel Butler's "The Historye of the Burmudaes or Summer
Isles," a work available to Smith in manuscript.[13] For the early pages,
which describe the islands and their plants and animals, Smith also uses
another manuscript account, Richard Norwood's "Insularum de la Bermuda Detectio."[14] A few pages concerning the shipwreck of Somers,
Gates, and Newport in 1609 are based on Sylvester Jourdian's *Plaine
Description of the Barmudas* (London, 1613). Smith writes of having
borrowed also from "divers others," some of whom he names; but, except
for some of the descriptions of the natural life of the islands, the story of
Henry May's shipwreck, and the last few pages on recent events (probably based on oral accounts), Smith seems to have used only the sources
noted. He made the book into a coherent, continuous narrative, though
on occasion his version is obscure because he condensed too much of what
his sources supplied.

Governor Butler's history is a book-length work that Smith trimmed severely; occasionally he supplemented it and brought it up to date. For example, he notes the names of six governors who succeeded Richard More (II, 359 ff.) and discusses the term of office of each, as Butler had not. Perhaps the most significant and revealing adaptation that Smith makes is his omission of Butler's long account of the power struggles in England, an indication of Smith's preference for action over problems of administration. The account of the case drawn up against Butler by Sir Edwin Sandys, which sheds light on the political context of English colonization, is all but omitted in the *Generall Historie*, where Smith merely wrote: "and withal, a strange and wonderful report of much complaint made against the Governor to the Company in England, by some of them returned in the last year's shipping" (II, 383).

On the other hand, the very practical Smith amplified Butler's brief comment on the colonists sent to the Bermudas: "so ill chosen they were (for they had been taken out of Newgate), that small hope of good was to be had of them . . ." (204). Smith put it more strongly: the colonists were "of such bad condition that it seemed they had picked the males out of Newgate, the females from Bridewell. As the governor found it his best course to grant out the women to such as were so greedy of wives and would needs have them for better for worse, and the men he placed in the King's castle for soldiers" (II, 381).

Smith's history of the Bermudas is a workmanlike job, except for a few spots where haste seems to have caused him to misrepresent his source. The book lacks both the strengths and the weaknesses of Book IV; it covers the subject better but without the sense of being authoritative. Because it is based on sources not available in published form until more than 250 years had passed, Smith made an important contribution to knowledge in this book.

Book Six

Like Book II, Book VI is based on Smith's earlier work. Entitled "The Generall Historie of New-England," it lacks effective organization because Smith's two earlier writings on New England do not fit neatly into a historical framework. Smith drew a good many pages of material from *A Description of New England* (1616), a mixture of description, adventure, narrative, and propaganda. This work was revised more thoroughly than the "Description" of Virginia had been for Book II, mostly to bring it up to date. The following insertion is worth noting.

1616 Version	*1624 Version*
From thence doth stretch into the sea the fair headland Tragabigzanda, fronted with three isles called the three Turks' heads. . . . (I, 339)	From hence doth stretch into the sea the fair headland Tragabigzanda, now called Cape Ann, fronted with three isles we called the three Turks' heads. . . . (II, 417)

Tragabigzanda and the Turks' heads recalled Smith's coat-of-arms, based on his experiences as warrior and slave in the Balkans and Turkey in his pre-Virginia years. Prince Charles had renamed at Smith's request many New England places listed on Smith's map, one for Charles's mother, Anne.

Some parts of the earlier version were rewritten—to improve them, apparently. Smith clarified and made more vivid the very obscure account in *A Description of New England* of his attempt to go to America in 1615 and then finding himself, because of a mutiny, on board a French vessel where he was abandoned "in his cap, breeches, and waistcoat, alone among the Frenchmen; his clothes, arms, and what he had, our mutineers shared among them . . ." (II, 431).

Smith next picked up from the revised and enlarged edition of *New Englands Trials* (1622). Because this work was written shortly before the *Generall Historie*, it was but slightly revised, mostly by the addition of a few paragraphs. Into the midst of the work he inserts (II, 443–53) a portion of "Mourt's" *Relation* (1622), an account of the Pilgrims now thought to be the work of Edward Winslow and William Bradford.[15] Smith chooses to revise his source at times, once in a quite effective fashion:

"Mourt's" Version	*Smith's Version*
we much fearing that if we should stay any longer, we should not be able to recover home for want of strength. (109)	our heads were as light for want of sleep as our bellies empty for want of meat. (II, 450)

After using a few more pages of *New Englands Trials*, Smith turned to Edward Winslow's *Good Newes from New-England*, published in London in the same year as the *Generall Historie*. He summarizes the whole of Winslow's book, omitting propaganda but moralizing a good deal, as when he added that an Indian who was hanged was "villainous." He next reprints, from *New Englands Trials*, a borrowing he had made there from John Dee's *General and rare memorials pertayning to the perfecte arte of navigation* (1577). Following a final borrowing, from Richard Whit-bourne's *Discourse Containing a Loving Invitation to Adventurers in the New-Found-Land* (1622), Smith presents his own account of the state of affairs in New England and a final bit of propaganda. Smith's hope was that fishing would now provide a sound economic basis for colonization, for fish "will afford as good gold as the mines of Guiana or Potassie [in Bolivia], with less hazard and charge, and more certainty and facility" (II, 474).

The *Generall Historie* Continued: *The True Travels*

Though Smith's reputation as a historian is considered to rest on the *Generall Historie*, there is more continuous historical writing in the second part of *The True Travels* (1630), a continuation of the *Generall Historie*. At first this part may appear to be mere padding, but Smith reported that, to prepare his accounts, he had "tired myself in seeking and discoursing with those returned" from America (III, 215). He combined oral reports into a series of unified chapters that stress the growing prosperity of Virginia, the Bermudas, and New England. Although Philip Barbour calls the account "humdrum, the writing apathetic,"[16] some engaging personal touches redeem the pages. Smith chides the Pilgrims, "whose humorous ignorances caused them, for more than a year, to endure a wonderful deal of misery, with an infinite patience, saying my books and maps were much better cheap to teach them than myself" (III, 221),[17] and he laments, bitterly, that "Those countries Captain Smith oft times used to call his children that never had mother, and well he might, for few fathers ever paid dearer for so little content" (III, 223).

As narrative, the extension of the *Generall Historie* that deals with English activities in Guiana is particularly effective. Smith tells with clarity and dispatch the little-known story, which began with Sir Walter Raleigh's work in 1595. What Smith's sources were is not certain, although part is derived from Purchas's *Pilgrimes*. Smith adds a personal note: he was to have been a member of an expedition to Guiana in 1605; but when the leader died, the voyage was not undertaken.

The story of the English colonies in the West Indies was Smith's next subject; his account seems to be based on written reports but they have not been identified. Smith had himself visited the isle of Nevis (he called it Mevis) in 1607, on his way to Virginia, and the description of that island is based on his recollection. The method of the *Generall Historie* is suggested here by an apology, perhaps half ironic, that Smith felt obliged to make at this point: "Because I have ranged and lived amongst those islands, what my authors cannot tell me, I think it no great error in helping them to tell it myself" (III, 235). Smith characteristically implies something a little larger than the truth: he had spent just over two weeks in the West Indies.

The *Generall Historie* Evaluated

The *Generall Historie* ends with no grand peroration. Indeed, knowing where it ends is difficult; for the conclusion of the continuation is an ending to only *The True Travels*, with an invitation to read more of Smith's adventures in the *Generall Historie*, here described as if it were another portion of *The True Travels*. The original six books have no real ending, for the preparation of the *Generall Historie*, especially that of the last pages, was hasty. But Smith did plan a book on an impressive scale, and through the first three books the *Generall Historie* is solid, carefully prepared. Richard Beale Davis usefully notes that from Smith's book "at least three major facts" emerge: "America, southern branch particularly, was a natural paradise; unfit and evil men, red and white, threatened to spoil this Eden; and the author alone knew what to do to prevent catastrophe."[18]

While the book has been called Smith's "Memoirs, his Apologia, and his Defense,"[19] it was intended to be something more. The frustration and bitterness of half a lifetime apparently prevented Smith from preparing what he thought he would produce: a memorial collection to promote the colonies with which he felt so closely identified. From the evidence of the rest of the *Generall Historie*, it appears that Book IV became the miscellany it is from personal pressures that Smith could not resist, not from plan. Having departed from his intention, he found it easy, under pressure of time, to use, without much revision, his not very appropriate earlier writing in Book VI. *The Generall Historie of Virginia, New-England, and the Summer Isles* is not a coherent and satisfying book because it reflects too often the damaged state of Smith's ego, though it should be remembered that the book would never have been written had not Smith been forced by circumstances to turn from the life of soldier to that of a writer.

Chapter Five

The Historian: *The Generall Historie*

All of Captain John Smith's writings are of historical value. In some, such as *A True Relation* and *A Description of New England*, Smith told the story of his own history-making adventures. In others, such as the *Generall Historie* and portions of *Advertisements For the unexperienced Planters of New England*, he compiled reports made by others, and, earlier, by himself. Even Smith's "Description" of Virginia is valuable as history, as Jarvis M. Morse long ago observed.[1] Smith's principal work of history is by common consent the *Generall Historie*. It is by far his longest work; in the modern edition of his writings, it occupies one large volume of the three-volume set. Of the *Generall Historie*, Smith's chief original contribution is in Book III, which contains about 22 percent of the whole.

When Captain John Smith, already an experienced writer, came to prepare for posterity an account of the years when he was in Virginia, he revised and amplified a report published some dozen years earlier; but, ironically, he made no use of his earlier, partial, on-the-spot account, *A True Relation*. Smith's source for the *Generall Historie*, *The Proceedings of the English Colony in Virginia*, originally published with his own "Description" of Virginia, does not name Smith as an author; but, since its compilers were his friends and admirers, he may have done some of the writing, as his revision suggests; and he definitely contributed information. Smith's intention was for the *Generall Historie* to be a collection and distillation of first-hand accounts; the compiler's role was to be that of collector of "the substantial truth from . . . a number of variable relations" (II, 44). Moreover, the writers of *The Proceedings* were full of praise of Smith; merely to reprint their compliments was surely very gratifying to Smith's ego.

A comparison of Book III of the *Generall Historie* and *The Proceedings* shows about 96 changes of more than a word or two. These include additions, deletions, and small modifications. The most important revisions are the additions, which consist of about 9,500 words of new material in a narrative of about 40,000 words. Ten new passages account for more than 8,000 words of the additions. Book III, with these changes, constitutes Smith's chief claim to importance as historian (as distinguished from compiler) if the *Generall Historie* is indeed Smith's greatest historical work.

Before the additions are examined, it will be helpful to consider the context of the preparation of the *Generall Historie* in Smith's life. Since 1617 he had been an armchair adventurer, but a very impatient one. Smith believed that his experiences in Virginia had taught him how to control the Indians; and, after the massacre of 1622, he had sought in vain to have the Virginia Company send him with soldiers to subdue them. When he prepared the *Generall Historie*, in the forefront of his mind was the conviction that he alone knew how to deal with the Virginia Indians in order to protect the English colonists. Many of the additions that he made to the 1612 account were motivated by these considerations.

Smith's Additions

The first significant addition deals with an event that took place after Captain Newport and the ships that had delivered the colonists had departed in 1608. A second president had succeeded Wingfield, and Smith had been appointed supply officer with the task of seeking food for the hungry colonists. For that purpose, according to the 1612 version, "he went down the river to Kecoughtan, where at first they [the Indians] scorned him as a starved man, yet he so dealt with them that the next day they loaded his boat with corn" (I, 211). The authors of *The Proceedings* apparently remembered the injunction of the Virginia Company of London "not to offend the naturals" and thus preferred not to explain how Smith dealt with the Indians.

But because Smith was undertaking his revisions after 1622—after the massacre—and was advocating a tough Indian policy, he wanted all to know how in one of the earliest encounters he had effectively frightened the Indians into submission. Smith's revised account, one of his most vivid pieces of prose, relates how he had landed his men—only six or seven—and had advanced on the village, where quantities of corn could be observed. Then the Indians attacked:

Sixty or seventy of them, some black, some red, some white, some party-colored, came in a square order, singing and dancing out of the woods, with their Okee (which was an idol made of skins, stuffed with moss, all painted and hung with chains and copper) borne before them; and in this manner, being well armed with clubs, targets, bows, and arrows, they charged the English, that so kindly received them with their muskets loaded with pistol-shot that down fell their god and divers lay sprawling on the ground; the rest fled again to the woods and ere long sent one of their Quiyoughkasouks [priests] to offer peace and redeem their Okee. (II, 144)

As in this passage, Smith often employed to good effect wry irony and lively pictures of his own heroism.

A few pages later occurs Smith's most famous addition in Book III, a 2,000-word passage about his captivity that replaces a much briefer description in *The Proceedings* account. This anthology piece is presumably reprinted so often because of its substance: every American should have the opportunity to read Smith's classic account of his rescue by Pocahontas. Many readers find the story quite different from what they had expected, for Smith makes clear from the very beginning that it was his own behavior that had saved him, not Pocahontas. While he was a prisoner, "many strange triumphs and conjurations they made of him, yet he so demeaned himself amongst them as he not only diverted them from surprising the fort but procured his own liberty and got himself and his company such estimation amongst them that those savages admired him more than their own Quiyouckosucks" (II, 146).

Smith saved himself by both bravery and quick-wittedness. As soon as he was captured, he asked to see the leader of the Indians; he filled the chief with wonder and admiration by demonstrating his compass and lecturing to him on cosmology. Then he added to the impression that he was a wonder worker by revealing the magic of written communication: he asked that some Indians be sent to Jamestown with a message from him; and, when they saw what happened, they thought that Smith "could either divine or the paper could speak" (II, 149). He also persuaded the Indians that an attack on Jamestown would be foolhardy because the settlers had huge guns and engines to guard them.

Smith's account emphasizes the savagery and the grotesqueness of the Indians. He tells how he was the focus of fantastic ceremonies: "presently came skipping in a great grim fellow, all painted over with coal, mingled with oil." "With most strange gestures and passions he began his invocation and environed the fire with a circle of meal; which done, three more such like devils came rushing in with the like antic tricks, painted half black, half red, but all their eyes were painted white, and some red strokes, like mustachios, along their cheeks. Round about him those fiends danced a pretty while, and then came in three more as ugly as the rest, with red eyes and white strokes over their black faces" (II, 149). When Smith was brought before Powhatan, the great chief, "more than two-hundred of those grim courtiers stood wondering at him, as he had been a monster, till Powhatan and his train had put themselves in their greatest braveries" (II, 150).

Smith makes no effort to make his story suspenseful; instead, he shows that he was so valiant that he could see the comic side of the episode. Even the description of Pocahontas's intervention has an amusing touch, an anticlimax that distracts the reader's attention from Pocahontas:

> Two great stones were brought before Powhatan. Then as many as could laid hands on him [Smith], dragged him to them, and thereon laid his head, and being ready with their clubs to beat out his brains, Pocahontas, the king's dearest daughter, when no entreaty could prevail, got his head in her arms, and laid her own upon his to save him from death; whereat the emperor was contented he should live to make him hatchets, and her bells, beads, and copper, for they thought him as well of all occupations as themselves. For the king himself will make his own robes, shoes, bows, arrows, pots; plant, hunt, or do anything so well as the rest. (II, 151)

Perhaps Smith was being tested; perhaps Powhatan had arranged in advance for his daughter to rescue Smith. Philip Barbour believed that the Indians had performed a "ceremony of which Smith had been the object . . . certainly a combination of mock execution and salvation, in token of adoption into Powhatan's tribe."[2] Responsible scholars have made these suggestions, but Smith said nothing. His concern was not really Pocahontas; it was Smith.

Bradford Smith, the biographer of Captain Smith, devoted several pages of his study to conjectures as to why the rescue story did not appear in Smith's early and longer account of his captivity, the *True Relation* of 1608. Of course, one can only guess at the answer. Similarly, one can only conjecture as to Smith's reason for including it in the *Generall Historie*. It may be here because one of Smith's special interests, both in Book II, the reprinted "Description of Virginia," and in the additions to Book III, is the relationship of the settlers and the Indians. It also serves as a memorial treatment of Pocahontas, who had died in England during her celebrated visit there, and whose bravery and devotion to the English Smith emphasized.

Only minor additions are to be noted for some pages after the captivity episode. The next long addition, about 300 words, is—like the first—a story that emphasizes how Smith treated the Indians with severity. In exploring Chesapeake Bay, Smith and his men met Indians at a place called Cuskarawaok. At first the Indians were hostile, but "The next day they came unarmed, with every one a basket, dancing in a ring, to draw us on shore." Smith suspected trouble: "there was nothing in them but villainy." He and his men, 14 in number, went ashore, "discharging five or six shot among the reeds." The outcome was that the Indians recognized the superior force of the English, and they therefore "became such friends [that] they would contend who should fetch us water, stay with us for hostage, conduct our men any wither, and give us the best content" (II, 165).

A few pages later, Smith added a good deal of information about a mine that he and his men had visited some 10 miles inland from the Potomac River. (The ore they obtained later proved worthless.) The purpose of the addition appears to have been to justify this exploring voyage: Smith noted that they sought to determine the natural resources of the area. In similar fashion, Smith added a few pages later two paragraphs on geography, including a dozen or so place-name references not included in the original account. Some of these additions are slightly egotistical, such as the reference to "Willoughby's River," named "in honor of the town our captain was born in" and Lord Willoughby, "his most honored good friend" (II, 172).

By far the longest addition that Smith made to his source is a section of about 3,300 words on the battles with the Rappahanocks and other Indians (II, 173–80).[3] *The Proceedings* reported simply that "we had much wrangling with that peevish nation; but at last, they became as tractable as the rest" (I, 232). In accounting for the change in attitude of the Indians, Smith wrote a lively story of four battles against them, all occasioned by treachery and ambushes. Some explanation of the pugnacity of the Indians was called for; and, with the capture of a wounded Indian (who was given careful medical assistance), an explanation was provided. He told them that the Indians have "heard we were a people come from under the world, to take their world from them" (II, 175). Smith did not question the validity of the Indian's view, nor was he at all defensive in his characterization of his adventures. He conceived of the Indians as inferior peoples obliged to recognize the superior status of the English. Mosco, an Indian guide who assisted the English in a variety of ways, was for Smith a childlike creature who took great delight in simple things: "we contented Mosco in helping him to gather up their arrows, which were an armful, whereof he gloried not a little" (II, 175).

This long addition is thus part of the argument that was indirectly urged by means of the additions in Book III and directly urged in Book IV: send Smith with troops to subdue the Indians, and force 500 Indians to work for the maintenance of the settlers. Besides the Indian argument, Smith emphasized in Book IV—as noted above—the fruitfulness of the years when he served in Virginia, in contrast to the more barren years that followed. In Book III, this theme is not very apparent, except in the next addition that Smith made to his source. It is purportedly a letter that Smith sent to the Virginia Company of London in reply to the instructions that Captain Newport had brought from the Company in September 1608. Though it is presumably not, as Barbour noted, a verbatim copy, Moses Coit Tyler gave it an extended treatment as one of Smith's three American works. Probably the substance of the letter that Smith actually sent was much like the one found in the *Generall Historie*. There is reason to suppose that the London leaders took cognizance of what Smith wrote, but if the original was as belligerent in tone, it surely must have offended some people. It is truly one of Smith's most important writings, an extremely revealing document in vigorous prose. Richard Beale Davis calls it "terse, bitter, ironic, bold."[4]

Smith begins with a kind of courtesy not likely to win friends: "I humbly entreat your pardons if I offend you with my rude answer" (II, 188). Then Smith argues that, though he had concealed nothing from the Virginia Company, the Londoners were in no position to send detailed orders to the colonists because such instructions are inevitably unrealistic. Presumably, the London officials thought that conditions in Virginia were so favorable to exploitation that the slim pickings of the first 15 months of settlement were the result of inactivity and lack of effort. The company had expected large, immediate results.

Smith answered the charges as a much unappreciated man: "Though I be no scholar, I am past a schoolboy." What do the Londoners know, he questioned, "but that [which] I have learned to tell you by the continual hazard of my life." Again, recognition of his own bravery inspired Smith to irony: he bitterly noted how ridiculous it was to suppose that the exploration of the James River beyond the falls could be made in a barge transported around the barrier. If Newport "had burnt her [the barge] to ashes, one might have carried her in a bag, but as she is, five hundred cannot, to a navigable place above the falls" (II, 188). The chief source of the colony's troubles was, according to Smith, Captain Newport, whom he made the villain of Book III. As one of the first members of the Virginia governing council, admiral of the fleet that brought the first settlers to Virginia, and chief supplier of goods, food, and colonists from England, Newport had authority and prestige. But Smith noted that, according to rumor, Newport and many officials of the London Company "maintain their families out of that you send us" (II, 189).

Smith's letter is a catalogue of explanations for the colony's failure to flourish: Newport, inadequate supplies, profiteering by the sailors of the supply ships, a lack of skilled labor. The writer is remarkably self-confident. Smith had no doubts—either in late 1608 or in 1624, one supposes—that, if he could have had his way, the colony would have flourished. And his demands were not great. His conviction that he knew what should be done is the source of the many half-humorous remarks that make the letter attractive despite the constant tone of irritation. Some of these remarks show that the Londoners were right in thinking the settlers lazy. "Though there be fish in the sea," wrote Smith, "fowls in the air, and beasts in the woods, their bounds are so large, they so wild, and we so weak and ignorant, we cannot much trouble them." (Smith's "we" is perhaps all the colonists except himself.) Captain Ratcliffe, a member of the governing council never very attractive to Smith, "is now called Sicklemore, a poor counterfeited imposture. I have sent you him home, lest the company should cut his throat. What he is, now everyone can tell you" (II, 189). Smith, one understands, had long known. This letter was an appropriate addition to the *Generall Historie*, for it does much to dramatize the plight of the colonists. It is one of the high points of the *Generall Historie*.

Smith's next addition was also motivated by his desire to demonstrate the worth of his Indian policy. The passage of some 220 words includes a paragraph on how Smith and his men learned to make camp in the woods in snowy weather, in "the open woods under the lay of a hill, where all the ground was covered with snow, and hard frozen; the snow we digged away and made a great fire in the place; when the ground was dried, we turned away the fire, and covering the place with a mat, we lay very warm" (II, 191).

The last extended addition made by Smith in preparing Book III is one of the most interesting, for it concerns Pocahontas. *The Proceedings* of 1612 had told the story of Smith's last visit with Powhatan and how Smith had bravely frustrated Powhatan's attempts to have him killed. For the *Generall Historie*, Smith added about 300 words to tell how Pocahontas, Powhatan's "dearest jewel and daughter," came in the "dark night" "through the irksome woods" to warn Smith of a new plot. The grateful captain sought to reward her, "but with the tears running down her cheeks, she said she durst not be seen to have any [gifts], for if Powhatan should know it, she were but dead, and so she ran away by herself, as she came" (II, 198–99).

Since the Smith–Pocahontas legend is well-known, one might suppose that the episode was added to fill out the picture of a relationship in which Smith took great pride. While there may have been something of this intention, in the context of Book III the reader is more likely to find it part of Smith's effort to persuade the English to adopt his Indian policy by presenting an example that demonstrated that his belief that the Indians were treacherous was well-founded. (Smith added only one other reference to Pocahontas, and it was made in passing.)

The most famous attack on Smith's veracity was made first in 1867 by the historian Henry Adams in a review essay on Smith in the *North American Review* and revised to attack Smith even more strongly when the essay appeared in a book. Adams, seeking to attract attention to himself, examined Smith's writings with particular attention to the Pocahontas story. He declared, "it is perfectly clear that the statements of the *Generall Historie*, if proved untrue, are falsehoods of a rare effrontery."[5] Adams implied that he had indeed proved them untrue. Because the story of Smith's rescue by Pocahontas is both the best-known event of his life and the one that has raised the most questions about his veracity, it is ironic that the same Henry Adams had made a very strong case for the plausibility of Smith's *Generall Historie* account in an 1861 letter to John Gorham Palfrey, who—according to Adams—had suggested to him "certain historic doubts as to Capt. John Smith and Pocahontas." Adams explained:

Smith had made many bitter enemies in Virginia and elsewhere, and if the story had been made up, it is hardly possible that it would not at once have been discredited, since five years are a mere nothing in such a case. But on the contrary it was received universally as true and created quite an excitement in London, naturally enough. In Virginia it seems to have been known from the first, for we are told from other colonists that the same Pocahontas continued to have a great affection for Smith and the English, and not only saved them from starvation but brought them information at the risk of her life. . . . Smith details his own interview with her in England and to my mind it bears the strongest marks of truth.[6]

Unfortunately, Adams chose to publish the attack without including even a hint of the position he set forth in the letter.

Others Changes in the *Generall Historie*

Besides these significant additions, all of which are effectively integrated into the narrative, Smith made many changes of smaller scope; most of these are merely the result of responsible editing. Smith added geographical details, indicated what the later consequences of activities had proved to be, made minor corrections, and added to lists of names. Some modifications reflect Smith's interests, for occasionally he inserted his name, and a number of small additions and changes were apparently motivated by egotism. For example, according to the 1612 account, the false charges against Smith had the effect of creating "a general hatred in the hearts of the company against such unjust commanders" (I, 207); according to Smith's revision, the consequences were also that Wingfield, the president, "was adjudged to give him [Smith] two hundred pounds, so that all he [Wingfield] had was seized upon in part of satisfaction, which Smith presently returned to the store for the general use of the colony" (II, 140). Of all Smith's revisions, this one seems most likely to be fiction; for two hundred pounds would have been a huge fine. But, in fact, Wingfield himself reported this fine as having been awarded "for slander." Smith's only inaccuracy was in dating: the incident occurred in September, when Wingfield was no longer president.[7]

Many of the modifications are denigrations of Captain Newport, who, according to Smith's addition, wanted him deposed from his position as president (II, 186). Smith criticized Newport's work as admiral: "we were at sea five months, where we both spent our victual and lost the opportunity of the time and season to plant, by the unskillful presumption of our ignorant transporters, that understood not at all what they undertook" (II, 143). The original version contains no such condemnation. Other changes make Smith seem very peevish. He omitted Newport's name when he referred to the presents sent to Powhatan.

1612 Version	*1624 Version*
Upon this Captain Newport sent his present by water. (I, 237)	Upon this, the presents were sent by water. (II, 184)

Another change speaks for itself:

1612 Version	*1624 Version*
And Smith, to make clear	But Captain Smith, to make clear

these seeming suspicions that the savages were not so desperate as was pretended by Captain Newport, and how willing	all these seeming suspicions that the savages were not so desperate as was pretended by Captain Newport, and how willing (since by their authority they would have
he was to further them to effect their projects (because the coronation would consume much time) undertook their message to Powhatan (to entreat him to come to Jamestown to receive his presents)	it so) he was to assist them what he could because the coronation would consume much time, he undertook himself their message to Powhatan, to entreat him to come to Jamestown to receive his presents. And where
	Newport durst not go with less than 120, he only took with
accompanied only with Captain Waldo, Master Andrew Buckler, Edward Brinton, and Samuel Collier. (I, 235)	him Captain Waldo, Master Andrew Buckler, Edward Brinton and Samuel Collier. (II, 182)

On the other hand, Smith adds kind words about Thomas Wotton, the surgeon; George Percy; and John Coderington. Indeed, Kevin J. Hayes has recently argued that a dominant theme of Smith's revision was the identification of the personal qualities needed to make the Virginia colony a success: "Smith never hesitated to credit individuals who possessed qualities that genuinely contributed to the establishment of a permanent colony."[8] Hayes goes so far as to entitle his study of Smith's revisions "Defining the Ideal Colonist."

The several speeches attributed to Smith are little changed. (To one, he added 15 words.) Perhaps he had looked them over before their publication in 1612, but it seems very likely that Symonds, the editor, was primarily responsible for these Thucydidean orations. From time to time, Smith added passages that reflect his values, especially his piety (such as "God be thanked" and "God doth know"). At several points Smith supplemented the original list of authors of the narratives and added, apparently, himself to the list as "I. S." (II, 153).

The *Generall Historie* as History

One other consequence of Smith's additions is worth noting. Most of the new passages are lively narratives full of details about the forest, the landscape and the Indians; crowded with action, often violent, these scenes are always vividly described. Smith's *Generall Historie* has been read and admired because it brings the reader very close to the America of the first English settlers. In Book III his work is generally responsible, intelligent, and useful; but it is also one-sided and conditioned by Smith's very personal motives. Smith's additions to Book III are, however, important contributions to our knowledge of early Virginia; and the book makes very good reading today.

Smith was a compiler, not a historian. To compare his work with that of William Bradford is to be unfair to Smith. He was much more like Hakluyt or Purchas; but, unlike these men, he dealt with what he knew firsthand (he was his own protagonist)—and he also added to the charm of his work the sense of his own attractive if opinionated personality.

Chapter Six
Pamphleteer and Poet

Having completed the *Generall Historie*, Smith could think of himself as a writer. The work he turned to next, *An Accidence or The Pathway to Experience, Necessary for Young Seamen*, was very successful in its time. It was not written from the motives that lie behind most of Smith's other writings; indeed, it seems to have been hack work. Besides, whether Smith had a means of livelihood during the 1620s is not clear, so one can conjecture that he needed money and could earn it from pamphleteering. He could still trade on the titles he had accumulated: "sometimes Governor of Virginia and Admiral of New England." (He had been in fact president of the Virginia governing council; later leaders were given the title of governor.) *An Accidence* and its sequel are the least important of Smith's writings, but some knowledge of the work and its composition contributes to an understanding of John Smith as man and writer.

An Accidence

Smith seems to have gotten his idea for *An Accidence* from Gervase Markham's *Souldier's Accidence, or An Introduction to Military Discipline*, which appeared in 1625, the year before Smith's *Accidence*. (The term *accidence* meant a discussion of the rudiments of the subject.) In the preface to Smith's 42-page quarto pamphlet—the first seamen's manual published in English—he explained his motives: because "many young gentlemen and valiant spirits of all sorts do desire to try their fortunes at sea, I have been persuaded to print this discourse. . . ." It was to serve, wrote Smith, "as an introduction for such as wants experience and are desirous to learn what belongs to a seaman" (III, 11). Later, in the preface to *True Travels*, Smith explained that his friend Sir Samuel Saltonstall had caused the book (or its augmented version) to be printed.

Very likely Smith undertook the book because of an increased interest in seamanship, for a naval war seemed likely after the government of King James had agreed in 1624 to help the Dutch republic in its war with Spain.[1] As the recent historian of navigation, D. W. Waters, has noted, Smith was very likely the best-qualified man in all England to undertake the composition of such a manual.[2] Smith was not a seaman, but his natural curiosity and practical bent must have led him to learn much from his experiences at sea: in the Mediterranean, around Morocco, twice across the Atlantic and back, travels as a captive on a French ship off the Spanish and French coasts, exploring Chesapeake Bay—nearly a year and half in all. From all this experience, which he summarizes in the preliminary "Epistle to the Reader," he had learned the importance of a good diet at sea, something better than the usual dried fish, salted beef and pork, beer, oatmeal, and cheese. In *An Accidence* he recommended that the food supply include currants, prunes, and roasted beef packed in vinegar. He described with feeling the hard lot of the sailor, especially "after a storm, when poor men are all wet and some not so much as a cloth to shift him, shaking with cold" (III, 29).

Most of *An Accidence* is little more than a series of lists: sails, winds, ropes, weapons. It is only occasionally that Smith captures the excitement of adventure at sea, as when he describes the terms of war in a bit of dialogue:

> "The ship's on fire. Cut anything to get clear, and smother the fire with wet clothes.
> "We are clear, and the fire is out, God be thanked."
> "The day is spent. Let us consult. Surgeon, look to the wounded. Wind up the slain, with each a weight or bullet at his head and feet. Give three pieces for their funerals."
> "Swabber, make clean the ship. Purser, record their names. Watch, be vigilant to keep your berth to windward and that we lose him not in the night. Gunners, sponge your ordinance. Soldiers, scour your pieces. Carpenters, about your leaks. Boats'n and the rest, repair the sails and shrouds. Cook, see you observe your directions against the morning watch." (III, 22)

Other passages here and there still make interesting reading, such as the list of duties of the marshal, who punished offenders by "ducking at yards arm, hauling under the keel, bound to the capstan or mainmast with a basket of shot about his neck, setting in the bilbos . . . (III, 16).

Intended to be practical, much of *An Accidence* is so condensed as to be almost unreadable, though it can be said to provide a vague, general impression of sea matters. Here, for example, is Smith's list of "the principal names of the timbers about the building [of] a ship":

First lay the keel, the stem and stern in a dry dock, or upon the stocks, and bind them with good knees. Then lay all the floor timbers, and cut your limber holes above the keel to bring the water to the well for the pump. Next your naval timbers, and bind them all with six-foot scarf at the least. The garbel strake is the outside plank next the keel. Be sure you have a good sufficient kelson, and then plank your outside and inside up, with your top timbers, but the lengths, breadths, depths, rakes, and burdens are so variable and different that nothing but experience can possibly teach it. (III, 17–18)

A Sea Grammar

In *An Accidence*, Smith noted in his preface, "For this small pamphlet, if I find you kindly and friendly accept it, I mean ere long more largely to explain the particulars" (III, 13–14). The work was an immediate success, and Smith began work on an augmented version. Once again Smith borrowed his title from Gervase Markham, who had now prepared *The Soldiers Grammar*. Smith called his new book, an 88-page quarto pamphlet that appeared in 1627, *A Sea Grammar, With The Plaine Exposition of Smiths Accidence for young Sea-men, enlarged*.

Philip Barbour has noted that, soon after the publication of *An Accidence*, someone called Smith's attention to Sir Henry Mainwaring's *Nomenclator Navalis*, there being several manuscript copies then in circulation. Mainwaring was an Oxford graduate of 1602 who turned to piracy and preyed on French and Spanish ships indiscriminately before receiving a royal pardon and being knighted in 1618. Not long thereafter he dedicated himself to writing a book for seamen that listed eight or nine nautical terms with hundreds of definitions. The earliest extant manuscript of this book was written between February 1620, and February 1623; but the most complete version dates from 1625. Smith seems to have seen a copy of this version and to have availed himself of it for both convenience and accuracy. (Sir Henry was a seaman; Smith was not.) In using Mainwaring's manuscript (which may have been unsigned) for reference, Smith borrowed many definitions verbatim or in abbreviated form; he incorporated them into his original plan, that of the earlier *Accidence*. The new book, *A Sea Grammar*, was a handbook designed to be read, whereas Mainwaring's was designed to be consulted. The latter was not published until 1644, when it appeared as *The Sea-mans Dictionary*. It was printed again twice, possibly three times. Smith's *Sea Grammar* went through four later editions or reissues before 1700.[3] It has a place of real importance as an indication of the state of knowledge of seamanship accessible in Smith's day.[4]

Smith acknowledged within his text another borrowing, a long "philosophical speculation" on the question of how deep the sea is. This passage is very different from anything else in Smith's writings, for it is full of references to Plutarch, Pliny, Aristotle, and other authorities. Only at the end, with some reluctance, did Smith reveal his source: "If you desire any further satisfaction, read the first part of *Purchas His Pilgrimage*, where you may read how to find all those authors at large. Now because he hath taken near one hundred times as much from me, I have made bold to borrow this from him, seeing he hath sounded such deep waters for this our ship to sail in, being a gentleman whose person I loved, and whose memory and virtues I will ever honor" (III, 95).[5] Both in his *Pilgrimage* and in his *Pilgrimes*, Purchas had borrowed, as has been noted, excerpts from Smith; he had died in 1626.

A Sea Grammar, a much more impressive work than *An Accidence*, is much fuller and more professional, thanks in part to Mainwaring. The highly condensed account in the earlier version of how a ship is built gave way to a whole chapter that is clear and precise. Chapters 9 and 13 are notably full of lively conversation. We read:

> "A sail!"
> "How bears she or stands she, to windward or leeward?"
> "Set him by the compass."
> "He stands right ahead, or on the weather-bow, or lee-bow."
> "Let fly your colors (if you have a consort, else not)."
> "Out with all your sails. A steady man to the helm. Sit close to keep her steady."
> "Give him chase or fetch him up."
> "He holds his own. No, we gather on him."
> "Captain, out goes his flag and pendants." (III, 101)

As Philip Barbour observes, *A Sea Grammar* is "a work of distinction in literary terms if one considers Smith's embellishment of the whole with 'you are there' immediacy" (III, 42).

Verses by Smith

Like several of Smith's other writings, *A Sea Grammar* is adorned with commendatory verses, seven in all. Such poems, which have been called "metrical puffs," are frequently found in sixteenth- and seventeenth-century books. One of the commendatory poems in *A Sea Grammar* is unusual in that it refers to the captain familiarly as "Jack Smith." "He's neither locksmith, goldsmith, nor blacksmith / But (to give him his right name) he's Jack Smith" (III, 53).

On two occasions Smith reciprocated with poems of his own. Since he was thought to have written only one extant poem, "The Sea Marke," these two recently discovered poems are of considerable importance; moreover, they show that Smith was a craftsman with considerable skill. The earlier of these appeared in 1627 in *An Armado, or Navye, of 103 ships and other Vessels; who have the art to Sayle by Land, as well as by Sea*, by John Taylor, a popular writer and famous London character, often known as "the water poet." Taylor's humorous pamphlet concerns such powerful "ships" as fellowship, courtship, and friendship. Taking his cue from Taylor, Smith used one dominant image in the poem. In mock-serious fashion, he warned the world of the danger occasioned by Taylor's fleet, so powerful that the gods of the sea, its monsters, and even the famous barriers such as Goodwin Sands off the coast of Kent are threatened. Among other aspects of Smith's art is his effective use of alliteration and sea terminology.

John Smith of his friend Master John Taylor and his Armado

> Arm, arm, arm, arm, great Neptune, rouse, awake
> And muster up thy monsters speedily.
> Boreas unto thy blustering blasts betake;
> Guard, guard yourselves, from Taylor's policy.
> Rocks, shoals, lee-shores, oh help them, Goodwin sands,
> For this new fleet runs over seas and lands,
> And's now so victualed, rigged, and yarely plies,
> It threatens all the waters, air and skies.
> Truth in his navy such a power doth lead
> The Devil, Hell, vice and all, the fleet may dreade.
> And well it may, if well you understand,
> So rare a fleet was never made nor manned. (III, 369)[6]

In *An Accidence* and *A Sea Grammar* Smith recommended to those interested in ships' guns "Master Robert Norton's expositions upon Master Digs." Earlier Norton had written a commendatory poem for the *Generall Historie* "to his much respected friend Captain John Smith." (Taylor had not honored Smith in this fashion.) Now Smith reciprocated when Norton's *The Gunner* appeared in 1628. His poem is much less striking than the one he had done for Taylor the year before: it is full of the commonplaces of the genre. But the often ungrammatical author of rough-hewn if vigorous prose did demonstrate with this poem that he was capable of turning out for a fellow soldier something at least competent.

In the due Honor of the Author Master Robert Norton, and his Work

> Perfection, if't hath ever been attained,
> In gunner's art, this author hath it gained
> By study and experiences, and he
> The fruit of all his pains hath offered thee,
> A present well befitting this our age,
> When all the world is but a martial stage.
> Let sweeter studies lull asleep and please
> Men who presume security, but these,
> Thy labors practiced, shall more safely guard
> Those that foresee the danger, th'other barred
> This benefit. We soldiers do embrace
> This rare and useful work, and o'er the face
> Of all the world, let thy fame's echo sound
> More than that roaring engine, and redound
> To th'honor of our nation that thy pains
> Transcends all former and their glory stains.

> Captain John Smith
> Hungariensis. (III, 370)

Chapter Seven
The Autobiographer

In his own time Captain John Smith's accounts of his adventures in the old world were questioned. They were satirized in a 1631 poem *The Legend of Captaine Iones*, by David Lloyd, based largely on Smith's autobiographical writings.[1] The historian Thomas Fuller noted in 1662 that "it soundeth much to the dimunition of his deeds that he alone is the herald to publish and proclaim them."[2] Charles Deane, addressing scholars 100 years ago, questioned Smith's reliability as an historian of Virginia, and Henry Adams followed suit, as has been noted. When in the 1890s Lewis Kropf, an amateur Hungarian historian, looked into Smith's account of his early years, *The True Travels*, he provided what appeared to be the ultimate condemnation of Smith's reliability. He doubted that Smith had ever been to eastern Europe, and he called the book "pseudo-romance."[3]

The best reason to doubt Smith's account is, that as John Seelye wisely explains, "the book has a fabulous quality suggesting that the whole cloth of truth has been patched out with colorful fabrications, and the result is a montebank appearance, a sort of clamorous advertisement for the author."[4] As a consequence, Smith's *True Travels*, until recently, has been much neglected. Countless popular articles have told the story of Smith's reputation, but even commentators on Smith's writings have had little to say about this story. One full account of Smith as a writer, that of Howard Mumford Jones, passes quickly by it, though Jones admires the work. Perhaps he might have said more, but, he noted, "Controversy will ever rage over the authenticity of the *True Travels*."[5]

Another extended general account of Smith's writing in this century, that of the judicious Jarvis M. Morse, carefully sidestepped the *True Travels*. Noting that the work is "partly fictitious," he argued that American scholars should not let doubts about it influence their judgment of Smith's other writings.[6] Thanks to the recent researches of Laura Striker, Bradford Smith, and especially Philip L. Barbour, Smith's account has been vindicated. Barbour's careful study led him to write that "nothing John Smith wrote has yet been found to be a lie."[7]

Smith's Adventures

The True Travels, Adventures, and Observations of Captaine John Smith, In Europe, Asia, Affrica, and America, from Anno Domini 1593 to 1629 appeared as a tall and handsome folio, decorated with illustrations— including Smith's coat of arms—in 1630, the year before Smith's death. In this thin volume with only 60 pages of text, Smith set forth his adventures in France, Italy, Hungary, Turkey, Russia, and Morocco. (The full title cited in the bibliography serves as a table of contents.) Before analyzing the book, however, a summary may be helpful.

Smith began the story of his life with a few lines on his family, his home, and his limited education: "He was born in Willoughby in Lincolnshire, and a scholar in the two free schools of Alford and Louth. [Smith used the third person throughout the account.] His father anciently descended from the ancient Smiths of Crudley in Lancashire, his mother from the Rickards at Great Heck in Yorkshire. His parents dying when he was about thirteen years of age, left him a competent means . . ." (III, 153). Later Smith was to associate with men of higher station than himself and was made to feel inferior, but recent research shows that his father was "the most important figure in Willoughby," a man who "would have enjoyed a considerable standing in the country-side roundabout."[8]

With only a little more than this abbreviated introduction, Smith plunged into an account of his adventures, which began about his sixteenth year with brief visits to France and Scotland and "three or four years" of military service in the Netherlands. These years were but preparatory to his great adventure in the wars being fought in southeastern Europe, for which he started out in 1600, around age 20. (There was a lull in the fighting in the Netherlands.) Cheated of his money and his belongings in France, with only partially successful efforts at revenge, he was cast into the sea by a group of Catholic pilgrims who considered him a Jonah. "Yet God brought him to that little isle where was no inhabitants, but a few kine and goats. The next morning, he espied two ships . . . put in by the storm, that fetched him aboard, well refreshed him, and so kindly used him that he was well contented to try the rest of his fortune with them" (III, 159).

Smith found himself on board a ship bound for Egypt, and he sailed along the African coast as far as Alexandria. On the return trip, Smith's ship engaged in a sea fight that led to adventures in the islands of the Mediterranean before he was finally able to reach Italy. Because all this time he was still headed toward the Hungarian wars, his passage appears to have been somewhat indirect. But Smith deliberately sought out new experiences to try his fortune, it appears, and so the time was not wasted.

Travels through Italy, mostly for sightseeing, preceded Smith's final arrival in Vienna. Becoming there a member of the army of the Holy Roman Empire, Smith soon made himself valuable by "an excellent stratagem": he explained how widely separated troops could signal their intentions to one another by torches. After extended fighting, Smith demonstrated his abilities further by the use of elaborate pyrotechnics, and he won a captaincy on the field. Then came what were surely among the great events of his life.

A Turkish officer had challenged the Christians to send forth a captain to "combat with him for his head." Smith was selected. The Turk

with a noise of hautboys entered the field well mounted and armed. On his shoulders were fixed a pair of great wings, compacted of eagles' feathers within a ridge of silver, richly garnished with gold and precious stones, a janissary before him bearing his lance, on each side another leading his horse, where long he stayed not, ere Smith with a noise of trumpets, only a page bearing his lance, passing by him with a courteous salute, took his ground with such good success that at the sound of the charge he passed the Turk through the sight of his beaver, face, head, and all, that he fell dead to the ground. (III, 172)

Smith next had to defeat—and to kill—the Turk's close friend. Finally Smith issued his own challenge and once again killed his opponent. Soon Prince Zsigmond Bathory learned of Smith's achievement and gave him "three turks' heads in a shield for his arms, by patent, under his hand and seal, with an oath ever to wear them in his colors" and "three hundred ducats, yearly, for a pension" (III, 175).

The defeat of the three Turks was a high point of Smith's adventures, and he celebrated his achievement by making good use of his coat of arms thereafter. It appears on the engraved title page of the *Generall Historie* and in a double-page engraving preceding Book II; it occupies a whole page just after the title page of the *True Travels* and appears again at the point where Smith tells of being honored by the Prince; and finally it serves as an illustration preceding the text of his *Advertisements For the unexperienced Planters of New England*. In 1625 Smith had it recorded at the College of Arms in London.

But Smith's adventures were far from over. Soon he took part in a great battle in which the Turks were victorious: "Smith, among the slaughtered dead bodies, and many a gasping soul, with toil and wounds lay groaning among the rest, till being found by the pillagers, he was able to live; and perceiving by his armor and habit, his ransom might be better to them than his death, they led him prisoner with many others" (III, 186). He was sent to Istanbul to be the slave of the "fair mistress" of Bashaw Bogall. (Smith calls her "Charatza Tragabigzanda." Though he thought this was her name, it simply means "girl from Trebizond.") She "took (as it seemed) much compassion on him, . . . but having no use for him, lest her mother should sell him, she sent him to her brother . . . in Tartaria" (III, 187). Extended descriptions of the Turks and Tartars fill several short chapters before one follows Smith to slavery north of the Black Sea. He found himself among many Christian, Turkish, and Moorish slaves, "and he being the last, was slave of slaves to them all" (III, 189). Smith reports that he was treated so badly that he "beat out the . . . brains" of his master and eventually escaped up the Don to Muscovy. Finally he was able to return to Hungary through southern Poland. Having had his fill of battle, he toured Germany, France, Spain, and Morocco; he describes the last of these in some detail. Once again he found himself in a sea fight, and once again he survived, finally returning to England after having been gone about four years. Here the story ends, for the second part of the *True Travels* is a continuation of Smith's *Generall Historie* (see chapters 4 and 8). The book does not provide, as the title page promises, an account of Smith's adventures to 1629. But the story he tells, though maddeningly interlarded with what might be called anthropological observations, is sufficiently eventful.

The Composition of the *True Travels*

The strange nature and history of Smith's little book is not apparent from this summary or even from a careful reading. The place to begin an investigation would seem to be the dedicatory epistle, where Smith informs his reader that he wrote the accompanying story of his life in response to a request by the antiquarian Sir Robert Cotton for "the whole course of my passages in a book by itself." In the writing of his autobiography, Smith is following, he reminds his readers, "many of the most eminent warriors and others; what their swords did, their pens writ." The book, Smith hopes, will "prevent . . . all future misprisions [mistakes or misunderstandings]" (III, 141–42).

This account is in fact somewhat misleading insofar as it suggests that the work is a new one. The basic story of Smith's life had appeared five years earlier, not as "a book by itself" but as a portion of the eighth book of *Purchas His Pilgrimes* (1625). The additions made for the 1630 version are the first chapter (a very condensed and rather obscure account of Smith's first 20 years), three chapters (14–16) on life in Tartary, and 11 chapters (18–28) that contain little autobiographical material. Many details not appearing in the 1625 version are found in the later one; but the relationship of these two versions is far from clear, even if something can be said about it. A further complication is that better than one-third of the earlier version is said in the *Pilgrimes* to be extracts from "The Warres of Transilvania, Wallachi, and Moldavia," described as "written by Francisco Ferneza, a learned Italian, secretary to Sigismundus Bathor the Prince." Philip Barbour, Smith's scholarly editor, theorizes that this work was a manuscript account of Smith's Transylvania experiences, used by both Purchas and Smith (III, 330–32).

Just how Smith came to write the Purchas version is not known, but presumably Purchas asked him for an account of his Near Eastern adventures for inclusion in Book VIII of the *Pilgrimes*, which deals with the Levant. What Smith supplied, Purchas probably trimmed and summarized in his usual fashion.[9] Purchas may also have suggested that Smith make use of Ferneza's "Warres" to provide authenticity, because the version of Smith's story found in *True Travels* closely follows Ferneza's work as presented in Purchas, much closer than the rest of *The True Travels* follows Purchas. (This portion includes the story of Smith's three successful jousts against Turkish opponents, by which he won the right to embellish his shield with three Turks' heads.) Smith repeated the attribution to Ferneza in the *True Travels* and noted that Purchas had made the translation. In the epistle "To the reader" in *An Accidence*, published in 1626, Smith recommended to those curious about his life his own *Generall Historie* and *New Englands Trials*, and "the life of Sigismundus Bathor, Prince of Translyvania, writ by his secretary, Francisco Ferneza" (III, 13). The problem of the composition of the *True Travels* would be nearer solution were Ferneza's book extant.

Smith wrote, according to my conjecture, an account of his life for the *Pilgrimes*, from which Purchas trimmed a good deal and to which Smith later added, in part by borrowing from other parts of *Purchas His Pilgrimes*. The differences between the cut version of Purchas and that found in the *True Travels* can be seen in the following parallel passages.

Purchas	*True Travels*
Opportunity casting him into the company of four French gallants well attended, faining to him	Opportunity casting him into the company of four French gallants well attended, faining to him the one to be a great lord, the rest his gentlemen, and that
they were devoted that way; over-persuaded him in the Low Countries, to go with them into France	they were all devoted that way; over-persuaded him to go with them into France to the Duchess of Mercury, from whom they should not only have means but also letters of favor to her noble Duke, then General for the Emperor Rodolphus in Hungary; which he did
with such ill weather as winter affordeth. (*Pilgrimes*, III, 341)	with such ill weather as winter affordeth. (III, 157)

Both versions include that part of the material said to be from Ferneza that tells of Smith's being granted a pension for his services in fighting against the Turks. In the *True Travels*, Smith supplied the patent by Zsigmond Bathory authorizing his coat of arms and a certificate by an English official to the effect that he has seen the patent and recorded it in the Register of the College of Arms.

More Borrowings by Smith

Another portion appearing in both versions, a short passage, is a borrowing from William Biddulph, a description of the Turks' food to be found only a few pages before Smith's story in Purchas, though it had earlier appeared in *The Travels of Foure Englishmen* (London, 1612). Presumably Purchas, a friend of Smith's, brought Biddulph's account to Smith's attention.

Smith augmented the earlier version by other extensive borrowings, as Barbour has noted. Chapters 14–16, life in Tartary, contain borrowings from two works found in the *Pilgrimes*: a thirteenth-century journal of Friar William de Rubruquis that had appeared in Hakluyt's *Principall Navigations*, and Martin Broniovius's *Description of Tartaria*, which appears in Purchas's *Pilgrimes*. A sample of Smith's borrowings follows:

Friar William	John Smith
Their houses wherein they sleep, they ground upon a round foundation of wickers artificially wrought and compacted together: the roof whereof consisteth (in like sort) of wickers, meeting above into one little roundel, which roundel ascendeth upward a neck like unto a chimney, which they cover with white felt, and oftentimes they lay mortar or white earth upon the said felt, with the powder of bones, that it may shine white. And sometimes also they cover it with black felt. The said felt on the neck of their house, they do garnish over with beautiful variety of pictures. Before the door likewise they hang a felt curiously painted over. For they spend all their colored felt, in painting vines, trees, birds, and beasts thereupon. (*Pilgrimes*, XI, 11)	The princes houses are very

artificially wrought, both the foundation, sides, and roof

of wickers,

ascending round to the top like a dove-cote; this they cover with white felt, or white earth tempered with the powder of bones, that it may shine the whiter; sometimes with black felt,

curiously painted

with vines, trees, birds, and beasts. (III, 192) |

One wonders whether Smith found life in Tartary so little different from what Friar William found it that he could use an account almost 400 years old. Perhaps the East was unchanging.

In writing the story of the Hungarian wars in which he was a participant, Smith used not only the aforementioned Ferneza, but also Richard Knolles's *General Historie of the Turkes*, probably in the huge volume issued as the third edition in 1621. For the portion on Africa (chapters 18–19) Smith used a whole range of sources, all of them conveniently at hand in Purchas's *Pilgrimes*. They include a translation of Lopez and Pigafetta's *Report on the Kingdom of the Congo* (in Purchas,

Volume VI), Robert Cottington's *Historie of Barbarie* (Purchas, Volume VI), Anthony Jenkins's "Voyage" (Purchas, Volume II), and John Leo's *A Geographical History of Africa* (Purchas, Volume II). These borrowed sections, like the one quoted above, are mostly descriptive of strange places and people.[10]

Smith referred to some of his sources, as when he advised his reader, "Of all these you may read in the history of this Edward Lopez, translated into English by Abraham Hartwell, and dedicated to John, Lord Archbishop of Canterbury, 1597" (III, 211). On another occasion, after borrowed descriptions of life in Tartary, Smith prepared his readers for more borrowings, but these are not supplied. "Many other strange and wonderful things are in the land of Cathay towards the Northeast, and China towards the Southeast where are many of the famous kingdoms in the world; where most arts, plenty, and curiosities are in such abundance, as might seem incredible, which hereafter I will relate, as I have briefly gathered from such authors as have lived there" (III, 199). Smith had touched Asia only at the Bosporus. If we reduce the *True Travels* to autobiographical portions that Smith seems to have written himself, we end up with a work of only about 12,000 words.

An Evaluation

Edward Arber, Smith's editor and an authority on sixteenth- and early seventeenth-century English literature, said of the *True Travels*, "in its clear, graphic, and condensed style, the narrative is among the very best written English books of travel printed in Smith's lifetime."[11] To the reader of travel writing by Smith's contemporaries, such as that in Purchas, this praise seems somewhat excessive. Smith's style is often far from clear because it is so condensed, and many of the most graphic passages are borrowed. John Gould Fletcher's comment is more valid: Smith's "literary style is, at best, the brief campaign-notes of a blunt soldier."[12] Smith truly did not always tell his story well, and he lost immediacy by using the third person to refer to himself. Perhaps he followed the example of Julius Caesar, whose writings he obviously knew. Like Caesar, he told nothing of his personal reactions to what he was and did, but sometimes his vivid accounts permit one to picture his actions.

Some of Smith's adventures are described in much less vivid language, and descriptions are so abbreviated as to be almost meaningless; other passages are little more than catalogues. Thus Smith led up to his service in the Hungarian wars with this summary: "Returning by Capua, Rome, and Siena, he passed by that admired city of Florence, the cities and countries of Bologna, Ferrara, Mantua, Padua, and Venice, whose gulf he passed from Malamoco and the Adriatic Sea for Ragusa, spending some time to see that barren broken coast of Albania and Dalmatia, to Capo de Istria, traveling the main [land] of poor Slavonia by Lubbiano [Ljubjana] till he came to Graz in Styria, the seat of Ferdinando, Archduke of Austria, now Emperor of Almania [Germany]: where he met an English-man and an Irish Jesuit, who acquainted him with many brave gentlemen of good quality, especially with the Lord Ebersbaught" (III, 162).

On the other hand, it must be said that the borrowings are intelli-gently made and that they usually add to the interest of the work. (The *Generall Historie*, mainly a compilation, attests that Smith was an expe-rienced borrower.) The quality of excitement that Smith maintains in the adventures themselves makes the work interesting despite his weak-nesses in other respects. The book provides a picture of Smith as a dashing and intrepid adventurer whose ingenuity was a great asset to his Hungarian colleagues and on occasion saved his life. Only once is Smith shown to be anything but a man of action. Here is our autobiographer at age 20, gathering his resources and adding to them after several years of warfare in the Netherlands and travels in France and Scotland:

Being glutted with too much company, wherein he took small delight, he retired himself into a little woody pasture, a good way from any town, environed with many hundred acres of other woods. Here by a fair brook he built a pavilion of boughs, where only in his clothes he lay. His study was Machiavelli's Art of War, and Marcus Aurelius,[13] his exercise a good horse, with his lance and ring; his food was thought to be more of venison than anything else; what he wanted, his man brought him. The country wondering at such an hermit, his friends persuaded one Signore Theodora Polaloga [Paleologue], rider to Henry, Earl of Lincoln, an excellent horseman and a noble Italian gentleman, to insinuate into his woodish acquaintances, whose languages and good discourse, and exercise of riding, drew him to stay with him at Tattersall. (III, 155–56)

Because Smith was an experienced and on occasion an effective writer by the time he wrote the story of his youth, as the passage just quoted demonstrates, it is a pity that he did not take greater care with his *True Travels*. Yet the book has noteworthy qualities. It is truly remarkable that Smith could report with considerable accuracy where he had been, though he wrote from memory nearly 25 years after the events, without the aid of notes or a journal and without much knowledge of foreign languages—some Italian, probably a fair knowledge of French, and a little German—with only the typical maps of his day, thoroughly inadequate ones, to jog his memory. (He does seem, however, to have picked up some help from books and printed maps.)

Though the literary quality of *The True Travels* is not consistently high, the adventures themselves still may charm readers as Othello's "hairbreadth 'scapes" charmed Desdemona—and they have the advantage of being true. Obviously, they were valuable experiences for John Smith, who won his title of captain (of 250 horse) in Hungary. (He was later made major, but he seems to have preferred the title of captain.) As he wrote in his last work, *Advertisements For the unexperienced Planters of New England* (1631), "The wars in Europe, Asia, and Africa taught me how to subdue the wild savages in Virginia and New England, in America" (III, 269). He could call himself an English gentleman, too; that is what Bathor's document calls him. Smith's story tells how he became self-reliant, tough, a leader of men, experienced in warfare. Having made himself valuable, he would not have to wait long to put his well-developed talents to work in Virginia, where once again he would achieve status above his blood and his education.

As autobiographer, Smith labored under a severe handicap: he lacked models. For Smith, "a recognized literary genre entitled 'autobiography' did not exist." The standard discussion of seventeenth-century English biography lumps the *True Travels* with other travel memoirs.[14] Philip F. Gura has suggested that Smith gave us "the first-person account of a life at least as interesting as Benjamin Franklin's," one which has, like Franklin's, "the virtue of being about a truly cosmopolitan figure who yet harbors a deep fondness for the American strand."[15] Recognition that as autobiographer Smith attempted an unusual task has been slow indeed.

Though he waited until near the end of his life to tell his story, Smith made interesting use of aspects of his early adventures in his American explorations. In a voyage up Chesapeake Bay, he names a peninsula Point Ployer after a French nobleman who had befriended him in Brittany, and in his New England travels he names a "fair headed" Cape Tragabigzanda after the girl whose slave he had been in Istanbul, and three islands off the headland Three Turks' Heads. Later, as noted elsewhere, Prince Charles renamed the cape, and posterity, ignoring Smith's exploits, soon gave the islands individual names: Thatcher, Milk, and Straitsmouth. (They are not to be confused with T. S. Eliot's "Dry Salvages" or Trois Sauvages.)

Smith himself characterized his career best: "how oft up, how oft down, sometimes near despair, and ere long flourishing" (III, 284). Both recognition and disparagement have been the story of his reputation since his death. Though all the facts can never be known, modern scholarship permits a sound assessment of Captain John Smith, his life and writings. To make the assessment, one must understand that peculiar autobiography, the *True Travels*.

Chapter Eight
The New England Writings

Because everyone knows the story of Pocahontas and because the *Generall Historie of Virginia* is often referred to as Captain John Smith's magnum opus, Smith is seldom identified with New England. Yet he gave it its name, and, as no less an authority than Samuel Eliot Morison emphasized, Smith "named this region New England and [was] for long the principal promoter of her settlement."[1] From 1614 to 1631, when he died, Smith devoted himself largely to the colonizing of New England. The theme of three of his works is New England, and one of these is his best.

A Description of New England

Englishmen had shown little interest in New England before 1602. (The story of the voyage of that year and later English visits to the area is discussed in chapter 1, and by Smith himself in Book I of the *Generall Historie*.) Smith visited New England only once, in 1614; and he stayed only three months. He explored the Maine and Massachusetts coasts; the story of this visit forms the basis of his third publication, *A Description of New England* (1616). Smith wrote this 79-page quarto during the summer and fall of 1615 while a captive on board a French ship. (He had been trying to return to America when he was captured.) Under these strange circumstances, "to keep my perplexed thoughts from too much meditation of my miserable estate, I writ this discourse . . ." (I, 357).

The importance of this little book is great because of its historic consequences and its crucial role in Smith's career as a writer. Of the former, Henry F. Howe argues that "neither Pilgrims nor Puritans would have reached Massachusetts when they did had it not been for Smith and his *Description of New England*. His was indeed the signal individual achievement in the founding of Massachusetts"[2]; and Richard Preston argues that "The *Description of New England* did much to focus attention on that part of the New World."[3] Of the latter, Philip Barbour writes that, with this propaganda pamphlet, Smith "found his true métier," for "this work is in a sense Smith's first solid opus—the first book in which we see his character as explorer, narrator, and ethnographer merged with his vision, his propagandist bent, and his retrospective self-discovery."[4] Smith sought to make his pamphlet as impressive as possible for propaganda purposes by dedicating it to Prince Charles, who had agreed to provide English names for the Indian ones on the excellent map of the area that accompanied the text. (Only three of Charles's names survive: Cape Ann, the Charles River, and Plymouth.)[5] Smith also addressed prefatory epistles to the King's Privy Council and to the companies of adventurers in London, Bristol, Exeter, and wherever; and he saw to it that nine poems, including ones by the notable poets George Wither and John Davies, precede and follow the text.

From these poems and prefaces comes an image of Smith that inevitably affects one's reading of the tract. From the poems, Smith appears to have been the victim of envy and malice (he is encouraged to "scorn the spite / Of Envy"), though a world-travelling patriot, the hero of Virginia, and a thoroughly honorable man. A former companion in Virginia praised Smith in these terms: "Some fight for wealth, and some for empty praise, / But thou alone thy country's fame to raise." One N. Smith wrote, "Hence damned Detraction: stand not in our way. / Envy itself will not the Truth gainsay" (I, 316, 314). In the preface Smith describes his book as "this rude discourse" and himself as ready to expose his "imbecility to contempt." He excuses himself for having been captured by pirates: "four men of war, provided as they were, had been sufficient to have taken Samson, Hercules, and Alexander the great . . ." (I, 310–12). From this time on, Smith's writings constantly remind the reader that he was a true hero victimized by circumstances.

The miscellaneous nature of Smith's book is suggested by its full title: *A Description of New England: Or the Observations, and discoveries, of Captain John Smith (Admirall of that Country) in the North of America, in the year of our Lord 1614; with the successe of sixe Ships, that went the next yeare 1615; and the accidents befell him among the French men of warre: With the proofe of the present benefit this Countrey affoords; whither this present yeare, 1616, eight voluntary Ships are gone to make further tryall.* The framework is basically chronological, but it is loose enough to permit Smith to include propaganda, specific suggestions concerning colonization, philosophizing, comments on his map and his values, and a document providing information about Smith's unsuccessful voyage of 1615. Some of Smith's best writing was occasioned by the enthusiasm with which he contemplated the colonization of New England. His frustration at his inability to be developing a colony there himself led him to pour his energies into writing.

The prose of *A Description of New England* is often quite different from anything found in Smith's earlier works. For example, in his efforts to stir his readers to recognize the virtues of colonies, he wrote the following artful passage of a decidedly philosophical cast.

Consider: What were the beginnings and endings of the monarchies of the Chaldeans, the Syrians, the Grecians, and Romans, but this one rule: What was it they would not do for the good of the commonwealth or their mother city? For example, Rome. What made her such a monarchess but only the adventures of her youth, not in riots at home but in dangers abroad; and the justice and judgment out of their experience when they grew aged? What was their ruin and hurt but this: the excess of idleness, the fondness of parents, the want of experience in magistrates, the admiration of their undeserved honors, the contempt of true merit, their unjust jealousies, their politic incredulities, their hypocritical seeming goodness, and their deeds of secret lewdness? . . . Then who would live at home idly (or think in himself any worth to live) only to eat, drink, and sleep, and so die? Or by consuming that carelessly [which] his friends got worthily? Or by using that miserably that maintained virtue honestly? . . . Or (to maintain a silly show of bravery) toil out thy heart, soul, and time basely, by shifts, tricks, cards, and dice? (I, 344)

Nothing in Smith's earlier writing prepares the reader for the rhetorical flourishes—the alliteration, the parallel constructions, the richness—of this passage.

Despite his moralistic approach, with its emphasis on hard work, honesty, and patriotism, Smith is fundamentally materialistic and bourgeois. He has much to say about the opportunity to get rich in the New World. "I am not so simple to think," wrote Smith, "that ever any other motive than wealth will ever erect there a commonwealth" (I, 346). His later impatience with the Pilgrims perhaps stemmed from the fact that their religious motives did fit his expectations. Elsewhere in *A Description of New England* Smith did invoke religion as a motivation for colonization, but in their context the words ring hollow: "Religion, above all things, should move us (especially the clergy) if we were religious, to show our faith by our works in converting those poor savages to the knowledge of God, seeing what pains the Spaniards take to bring them to their adulterated faith" (I, 350). Besides patriotism, wealth, and religion, Smith suggested another motive for going to New England: it was a pleasant place in which to live, his preferred place, where everyone, young or old, rich or poor, could be happy. A gentleman might have all the pleasures that hawking and hunting provide, and for the ordinary workman, "What pleasure can be more than (being tired with any occasion ashore) in planting vines, fruits, or herbs, in contriving their own grounds, to the pleasure of their own minds, their fields, gardens, orchards, buildings, ships, and other works, etc., to recreate themselves before their own doors, in their own boats upon the sea, where man, woman, and child with a small hook and line, by angling may take divers sorts of excellent fish at their pleasures?" (I, 347). Smith's insistent emphasis on ownership is not to be ignored. As Stephen Innes has shown, "Few questions were so compelling to Englishmen in the early modern era as the ownership of one's 'own labor.'" He notes that, significantly, "John Smith's linkage of control of both one's labor and one's land was an attempt to speak to the aspirations" of two distinct groups: those who were to come from metropolitan areas, "impecunious and youthful artisans" who arrived as indentured servants, and those from the provinces, who came as substantial families. Both were appealed to, and it was these two groups that populated the American colonies. Indeed, Innes notes, America was to give people what Smith had prophesied, "a chance they otherwise would not have had."[6] (One wishes that Smith's admiration of the climate of New England, another subject to which he gives special attention, could have undergone the test of a typical winter; for his visit was in late spring and summer.)

It is perhaps difficult to reconcile the conflicting motives for colonization that Smith urges, and sometimes the result is a kind of aimlessness. But the virtues of Smith's little book heavily outweigh its limitations: though Smith's visit to New England had been a brief one, he was still able to provide a precise description of the coastline both in *A Description of New England* and on the map (no easy feat, as other descriptions and maps of the time demonstrate); the Indian names or his own for the most important topographical features; and a very full list of the flora and fauna, including what seems to be the first mention of the muskrat by a visitor to New England. Whereas earlier colonizing efforts had been directed at Maine, he saw that Massachusetts was the best place in New England for settlement; to him, it was "the paradise of all those parts" (I, 340).

Most of Smith's descriptions of the coast, Indian tribes, wildlife, and vegetation consist of little more than a catalogue. At times, however, Smith offers charming pictures, such as these:

I made a garden upon the top of a rocky isle [probably Monhegan Island] in 43 ½ [degrees latitude], four leagues from the main[land], in May, that grew so well as it served us for sallets in June and July. (I, 334)

Angoam [Agawam] is the next. This place might content a right curious judgment, but there are many sands at the entrance of the harbor, and the worst is, it is embayed too far from the deep sea. Here are many rising hills, and on their tops and descents, many corn fields and delightful groves. (I, 339)

[There is] no river where there is not plenty of sturgeon or salmon or both, all which are to be had in abundance, observing but their seasons. But if a man will go at Christmas to gather cherries in Kent, he may be deceived, though there be plenty in summer. So here, these plenties have each their seasons, as I have expressed. (I, 343)

Smith was not only an excellent explorer; he was also a thoughtful creator of seemingly sound and certainly concrete proposals for colonization. Eva G. R. Taylor asserts that "Nothing could be more judicious than Smith's proposals for organized settlement" of New England.[7] Smith knew from his Virginia experience that "it is not a work for everyone, to manage such an affair as makes a discovery and plants a colony." He knew that it required "all the best parts of art, judgment, courage, honesty, constancy, diligence, and industry to do but near well"; that "some are more proper for one thing than another, and therein are to be employed"; and that "nothing breeds more confusion than misplacing and misemploying men in their undertakings" (I, 327).

Smith thought that poor people, including children, could be advantageously shipped to America to serve as laborers. Many Londoners considered that plagues were caused by conditions among the poor, and in 1617, £500 was raised to ship 100 poor children to Virginia, where they were to be apprenticed until age 15.[8] Smith tried to be specific. He specified the profits to be realized from fishing and offered ideas on later improvements of the arrangement. The process would, in his opinion, result in substantial immediate profits; but patience would be required for real success. As Smith puts it in one of his most effective passages:

if twenty years be required to make a child a man, seven years limited [to prepare] an apprentice for his trade; if scarce an age be sufficient to make a wise man a statesman, and commonly a man dies ere he hath learned to be discreet; if perfection be so hard to be obtained, as of necessity there must be practice as well as theoric, let no man much condemn this paradox opinion, to say that half seven years is scarce sufficient for a good capacity to learn in these affairs how to carry himself, and whoever shall try in these remote places the erecting of a colony shall find at the end of seven years occasion enough to use all his discretion, and in the interim all the content, rewards, gains, and hopes will be necessarily required. . . . (I, 349)

This passage continues on luxuriantly, at times all but getting out of hand, as Smith piles up strings of nouns and clauses.

On the basis of his own experienced leadership—he who had "learned there is a great difference betwixt the directions and judgment of experimental knowledge and the superficial conjecture of variable relation" (I, 351–52)—Smith believed he could make a successful colony with soldiers and workmen. As he conceived it, the social structure of the colony would differ in significant ways from that of the mother country; for America would permit the development of the self-made man. "Who can desire," he wrote, "more content that hath small means or but only his merit to advance his fortune, than to tread and plant that ground he hath purchased by the hazard of his life?" (I, 343) "And here are no hard landlords to rack us with high rents or extorted fines to consume us" (I, 332).

In 1615, Smith was given the opportunity to do what he had in mind; but, after having had his would-be colonists reduced to a mere 16, his plans were, as has been noted, interrupted by pirates, to Smith's immense irritation and embarrassment. *A Description of New England* ends with an account of these misadventures that includes one of Smith's most vivid pictures of himself. For months he had been held captive by French pirates; now on board ship in a French port.

In the end of such a storm that beat them all under hatches, I watched my opportunity to get ashore in their boat, whereinto, in the dark night, I secretly got, and with a half pike that lay by me, put adrift for Rat Isle, but the current was so strong and the sea so great, I went adrift to sea, till it pleased God the wind so turned with the tide that although I was, all this fearful night of gusts and rain, in the sea the space of twelve hours, when many ships were driven ashore and divers split (and being with sculling and bailing the water tired, I expected each minute would sink me), at last I arrived in an oozy isle by Charowne [the Charente River], where certain fowlers found me near drowned and half dead with water, cold, and hunger. (I, 358)

This passage is typical of Smith: confused sentence construction that still does not prevent the experience from being realized in words.

Smith then briefly told the story of his return to England and concluded with a final exhortation to himself and his readers to overcome their "idleness and ingratitude to all posterities, and the neglect of our duties in our piety and religion we owe our God, our King, and country" (I, 361).

An additional page inserted in some copies of the pamphlet lists the Indian place names or new ones supplied by Smith, and in a second column the ones that Prince Charles had substituted. Smith's *Description of New England* appeared in only one edition as a pamphlet, but the map was frequently reprinted, and he incorporated the text into Book VI of the *Generall Historie*. Smith's most important contributions to American place names deserve special mention. Throughout his pamphlet, Smith referred to the area he had visited as New England. It had formerly been called the northern part of Virginia or Norumbega; but Smith's *Description of New England* and his map, with Prince Charles's confirmation, gave it the name it still has. Smith did not invent the name Massachusetts, but he picked up the name of the Indian tribe and applied it to the region now called by that name, or rather to the coastal portion of the region.[9]

New Englands Trials

Smith continued to seek to establish a colony in America. In 1617, probably under the auspices of the North Virginia Company, he prepared to cross the Atlantic with three ships; but he was again frustrated. Contrary winds kept the ships from leaving Plymouth harbor, and after three months' delay, the voyage was abandoned. Smith's title—Admiral of New England—proved to be all but a mockery, for of course he never went to New England again.[10]

The year after this stalemate, 1618, Smith wrote to Lord Bacon to request a £5,000 investment in a colony in New England. (The letter is included in the Barbour edition of the *Works of Smith*.) Again his plans called for profits from fishing. Though no colonists had arrived in America since Smith's expeditions off the coast, he cited a good deal of evidence. This time he described his 1614 voyage as a financial success, with a profit of "near the value of 1500 pounds" (I, 380) though his 1616 report does not make clear that it had made a profit. Achieving no results with this letter,[11] Smith decided to revise and publish it in order to appeal to other possible sponsors. *New Englands Trials. Declaring the successe of 26. Ships employed thither within these six years: with the benefit of that Countrey by sea and land: and how to build three score sayle of good ships, to make a little Navie Royal* appeared in late 1620. (By *trials*, Smith meant "things tried.")

Smith presented this promotional tract, according to the *Generall Historie*, "with a great many maps both of Virginia and New-England . . . to thirty of the chief companies in London at their halls, desiring either generally or particularly (them that would) to embrace it, and by the use of a stock of five thousand pound to ease them of the superfluity of the most of their companies that had but strength and health to labor" (II, 442). As Wilberforce Eames has shown in his Smith bibliography, copies were addressed to "the Right Honorable Adventurers to all discoveries and plantations, especially to New England," to the company of fishmongers (and presumably other guilds), to Chief Justice Edward Coke, and to Sir John Egerton.[12] Again Smith found no backers.

The first edition of *New Englands Trials* is a collection of very miscellaneous materials. After a brief introduction on New England's location, geography, and climate, Smith presents statistics on the profits that had been made from fishing. Then he notes the advantages of New England for fishing and cites 10 proofs of these advantages in the form of brief factual reports on successful fishing voyages. Then comes an autobiographical passage. Smith's sense of mistreatment and neglect, reflected in the prefaces and poems of *A Description of New England*, is in the background of the text of that work; in *New Englands Trials* it comes to the foreground.

Having cited the virtues of New England and the successful fishing ventures made there, Smith felt obliged to face the question of why he himself had done so little. Why did he make "no more use of it and rest so long without employment"? (I, 400). Smith answers by reporting his great sacrifices of time and money on behalf of both Virginia and New England. With great bitterness he reports, "I never had power and means to do anything (though more hath been spent in formal delays than would have done the business) but in such a penurious and miserable manner, as if I had gone a-begging to build an university, where, had men been as forward to adventure their purses as to crop the fruits of my labors, thousands ere this had been bettered by these designs" (I, 401). In the earlier book on New England, the autobiographical aspect was appropriate. Smith was, after all, describing what he uniquely knew. But his zeal to colonize the New World was marred by his inability to subordinate his own disappointment. This flaw mars both *New Englands Trials* and the *Generall Historie*. It was inappropriate, therefore, for Smith to complain of "everyone so regarding his private that it is hard to effect public good" (I, 402).

Smith next urged his colonizing plan, which was, as it had been before, to combine fishing expeditions with colonizing. To this end, Smith suggested that Britain had had a historic interest in fishing. His authority was John Dee's *General and rare memorials pertayning to the Perfect Arte of navigation* (1577), which Smith referred to as "British Monarchie," the title of the first part. He used almost everything else that came to hand with little sense of discrimination or plan: geographical description, catalogues of fish, requests for funds, quotations. The 1620 version is not marked by any particular literary excellence; indeed, it seems to have been hastily thrown together.

A second edition of *New Englands Trials* was prepared in October 1622 and published soon after with dedications to Prince Charles and to the adventurers. This edition added to the first an account of recent events. It is half again as long as the first edition, 14 pages to the first edition's eight. The 1622 version contains interesting new material, but it too seems patched together. Smith added three paragraphs on the Plymouth Colony, its adventures and misadventures, set forth in a simple and factual manner, though he did not deny himself the opportunity of mentioning that the colonists were "for want of experience ranging to and again, six weeks before they found a place they liked to dwell on" (I, 429). (Had *he* guided them, they would have had no problems.) Later he was to chide them for seeking "to save charges" by trying "their own conclusions, though with great loss and much misery" (III, 282). Smith also included in the 1622 edition a letter confirming his report on the wealth of New England in foodstuffs. This letter made an observation that Smith frequently emphasized: the colonists "are all freeholders," wrote William Hilton; "the rent day doth not trouble us" (I, 431).

Another letter from New England, reporting that the colonists there were "more wary" of the Indians since the massacre in Virginia in March 1622, led Smith to an extended and significant digression—eight paragraphs on Virginia, which could be considered propaganda on his own behalf. When Smith rehearses his experience with Virginia Indians, his writing comes alive. He reports on his prowess as military leader and Indian fighter. "When I had ten men able to go abroad, our commonwealth was very strong. With such a number I ranged that unknown country fourteen weeks. I had but eighteen to subdue them all, with which great army I stayed six weeks before their greatest king's habitation, till they had gathered together all the power they could" (I, 432).

Smith had already proposed earlier in 1622 that he be put in charge of a group of soldiers to prevent further massacres. Later in the *Generall Historie*, he tells the story of his offer and the neglect that it met. Yet now he felt that, despite the lack of recognition that his efforts brought him, he might still speak of the American colonies as "my children, for they have been my wife, my hawks, my hounds, my cards, my dice, and in total my best content" (I, 434). He wanted very much to return. This digression also includes Smith's first published account of his rescue by Pocahontas. (In the *Generall Historie* he was to include a letter about how she had saved him; this letter he dated from 1616.) Here he writes merely that, when the Indians had captured him, "God made Pocahontas, the king's daughter, the means to deliver me" (I, 432).

The enlarged *New Englands Trials* is still very slight; and, except for the autobiographical passage, its literary value is not great. Historically, the pamphlet is more important; for it provides a full record of English voyages to New England from 1616 to 1622. Smith's careful distribution of copies of the pamphlet presumably did something toward directing English attention to New England. (The first edition, it should be noted, did not appear until after the Pilgrims had departed.)

New England in the *Generall Historie*

In the *Generall Historie*, Smith reprints in slightly revised form his two earlier writings on New England and abridgments of other men's writings (see the discussion in chapter 5). He also adds a few comments, such as a paragraph on the comparative worth of gold and silver mines and of fish. The continuation of the *Generall Historie*, published as the second part of the *True Travels* (1630), includes an important chapter on "The proceedings and present estate of New England since 1624 to this present 1629." This chapter is more strictly autobiographical than *New Englands Trials*. Throughout its survey of the recent history of New England, one is never permitted to forget whose voice is behind the words.

Smith begins by emphasizing that, before his 1614 visit, New England was "then reputed by your westerlings [the Plymouth Company] a most rocky, barren, desolate desert, but [from] the good return I brought from thence, with the maps and relations I made of the country, which I made so manifest, some of them did believe me." While some voyages were made to New England, Smith and his friends "consumed many hundred pounds among the Plimothians, who only fed me with delays, promises, and excuses, but no performance of anything to any purpose" (III, 221). It is only too apparent that Smith bitterly resented this treatment, especially since the colonization of New England was, according to his own report, gaining momentum without him. (He noted the departure in 1629 of 350 colonists, the first large contingent of the Massachusetts Bay Company.) But, he insists, his role in the colonies had been crucial; once again he calls them his children: "Those countries Captain Smith oft times used to call his children that never had mother, and well he might, for few fathers ever paid dearer for so little content" (III, 223). (Smith seems even more self-pitying when he writes of himself in the third person.) Even yet, he urges, his presence in America was indispensable:

For yet those countries are not so forward but they may become as miserable as ever, if better courses be not taken than is, as this Smith will plainly demonstrate to his Majesty or any other noble person of ability, liable generously to undertake it: how within a short time to make Virginia able to resist any enemy, that as yet lieth open to all, and yield to the King more custom within these few years in certain staple commodities than ever it did in tobacco, which now not being worth bringing home, the custom will be as uncertain to the King as dangerous to the plantations. (III, 223)

In 1629, when Smith wrote the above, he was still eager to return to America, though he was nearly 50. He was somewhat less conscious, however, of his frustrations and more aware of his accomplishments; in the concluding (if penultimate) chapter of the *True Travels*, he notes that among his adventures was bringing "our New England to the subjection of the Kingdom of Great Britain" (III, 237–38).

Advertisements For the unexperienced Planters of New England

John Smith's final work on New England was his last book: *Advertisements For the unexperienced Planters of New England, or any where. Or, the Path-way to experience to erect a Plantation* was written in October 1630 and published in 1631. Though only 40 pages long, from a literary point of view, it is doubtless Smith's best book. He wrote it by interrupting the composition of what would presumably have been a big book, perhaps like the *Generall Historie*; he describes it as "my history of the sea" (III, 290). He died before he could finish it, and the work was lost, a great pity because he was beginning to achieve considerable literary skill.

The *Advertisements*, a 48-page quarto pamphlet, provides few facts about Smith that he had not set forth already; but the personality of the author shines through more attractively than anywhere else. A. L. Rowse has argued that Smith "is a writer by nature: the very assertion of personality shows it, against dull dogs."[13] But elsewhere Smith's writings are often not enlivened by a sense of the author's personality but marred by his tone of victimized hero. The *Advertisements*, though even fuller of braggadocio than Smith's other works, shows much more of the spirit that is revealed at points in the second part of the *True Travels*: a sense of its own triumph and success. Here is his outlook, vigorously expressed:

Having been a slave to the Turks, prisoner amongst the most barbarous savages, after my deliverance commonly discovering and ranging those large rivers and unknown nations with such a handful of ignorant companions that the wiser sort often gave me [up] for lost; always in mutinies, wants, and miseries, blown up with gunpowder; a long-time prisoner among the French pirates, from whom escaping in a little boat by myself and adrift all such a stormy winter night when their ships were split, more than an hundred thousand pound lost we had taken at sea, and most of them drowned upon the isle of Ré, not far from whence I was driven on shore in my little boat, etc. And many a score of the worst of winter months lived in the fields, yet to have lived near thirty-seven years in the midst of wars, pestilence, and famine, by which many an hundred thousand have died about me, and scarce five living of them [that] went first with me to Virginia, and see the fruits of my labors thus well begin to prosper. Though I have but my labor for my pains, have I not much reason both privately and publicly to acknowledge it and give God thanks, whose omnipotent power only delivered me, to do the utmost of my best to make his name known in those remote parts of the world and his loving mercy to such a miserable sinner. (III, 284–85)

This passage reveals a great deal about Smith. Once the reader has worked his way through the syntax, the reader is struck by the romanticized view of himself that Smith had developed in the 15 years since his last real adventure. The passage also shows that his imagination offered him considerable consolation and comfort in his pain and bitterness and suggests that he had a new appreciation of the importance of religion, which also seems to have provided him with consolation. This impression is strengthened by the fact that the *Advertisements* was dedicated to the Archbishops of Canterbury and York, "to leave testimony to the world how highly I honor as well the miter as the lance" (III, 263).

Smith's newly found piety, if that is what it was, is reflected in the chapter devoted to religion in the *Advertisements*. Whereas earlier Smith had disparaged religion as a basis for colonization or had given only cursory attention to it, he now adds a new ingredient to his formula for a successful colony: the church. Smith argues that religion is an indispensable instrument of order, a preventer of factionalism: he describes at some length the religious practices of the Jamestown colonists of his days in Virginia. The most important evidence that religion was now of considerable importance to Smith and helped him to develop a more philosophic attitude toward his career is the striking and powerful poem that prefaces the *Advertisements*. Presumably it is Smith's, and it surely sets forth in the first two stanzas an attitude that was very much his.

The Sea Mark[14]
Aloof, aloof, and come no near;
　　the dangers do appear;
Which if my ruin had not been
　　you had not seen:
I only lie upon this shelf
　　to be a mark to all
　　which on the same might fall
That none may perish but myself.

If in or outward you be bound,
　　do not forget to sound.
Neglect of that was cause of this,
　　to steer amiss.
The seas were calm, the wind was fair,
　　that made me so secure,
　　that now I must endure
All weathers be they foul or fair.

After thus indulging in self-pity, in the last stanza Smith finds consolation:

The winter's cold, the summer's heat
　　alternatively beat
Upon my bruised sides, that rue
　　because too true
That no relief can ever come.

But why should I despair,
　　being promised so fair
That there shall be a Day of Doom. (III, 265)

The defeated adventurer rested, assured that his achievements were responsible for the colonization of the New World and that recognition would come in time, though not in his lifetime. Smith would have been pleased to be denominated what J. A. Leo Lemay calls him, "the greatest single founder of the English colonies in America."[15]

In the *Advertisements*, Smith continued his disparagements of the Separatists of the Plymouth Colony; he particularly disliked "their pride, and singularity, and contempt of authority. Because they could not be equals, they would have no superiors" (III, 286). He seems to have been oblivious that Winthrop and the men of Massachusetts Bay were Puritans, for he reports that Winthrop and his council had been put "to their utmost wits" by some who "could not endure the name of a bishop, others not the sight of a cross nor surplice, others by no means the Book of Common Prayer" (III, 292–93). These had all returned to England or moved to Plymouth, according to Smith's story.[16]

The book has many expressions of both admiration and advice for the Massachusetts settlers. Smith argued the importance of making America a land of opportunity for all, a place where a servant might become as prosperous as his master had been in the Old Country. He advised strongly against excessive taxation: "have a care that all your countrymen [that] shall come to trade with you be not troubled with pilotage, buoyage, anchorage, wharfage, custom, or any such tricks as hath been lately used in most of new plantations, where they [the leaders] would be kings before their folly, to the discouragement of many . . ." (III, 298).

The contents of the *Advertisements* are, however, too varied to merit what Smith at one point called it, "a memorandum of my love" to Governor Winthrop and the other leaders of the Massachusetts Bay Colony, "to make your plantations so near [contiguous?] and great as you can" (III, 287). Rather the theme is, once again, the desirability of colonization and the best methods for carrying it on, with New England, not Virginia, receiving Smith's special attention here. The autobiographical ramblings do not, this time, give the impression of having been inserted from egocentrism or to pad out a thin book, for they are all related to Smith's theme. Each of the 15 chapters has some unity, and the middle chapters tell in almost chronological order the story of the exploration and settlement of New England. The new, less defensive John Smith is most apparent in the three chapters—12, 13, and 15—in which he hands on to colonists and would-be colonists practical advice on farming, building forts, preparing for military combat, putting the

Indians to work, and selecting good leaders. Here he does not protest too much.

Smith had mellowed and was now in much better control of himself and of the materials he wished to organize into a book. At times, he demonstrated a wonderfully disciplined sense of irony—not just in a sentence or two but in whole paragraphs. In this tone, he treats what had been particularly annoying to him: the demands made on him as president of the governing council in Virginia by the controlling officials in London. He had responded by seeing to it that each ship returning to England was freighted with "only some small quantities of wainscot, clapboard, pitch, tar, rosin, soap-ashes, glass, cedar, cypress, black walnut, knees for ships, ash for pikes, iron ore none better, some silver ore but so poor it was not regarded—better there may be, for I was no mineralist—some sturgeon, but it was too tart of the vinegar (which was of my own store, for little came from them which was good), and wine of the country's wild grapes, but it was too sour, yet better than they sent us any in two years or three but one hogshead of claret." In the meantime, Smith was "only spending my time to revenge my imprisonment upon the harmless innocent savages, who by my cruelty I forced to feed me with their contribution and to send any [who] offended my idle humor to Jamestown to punish at mine own discretion." These actions, the London officials charged, were "things clean contrary to my commission, whilst I and my company took our needless pleasures in discovering the countries about us, building of forts and such unnecessary fooleries, where an eggshell (as they writ) had been sufficient against such enemies" (III, 271).

Smith's account of what he had shipped to England involves considerable exaggeration, but it is much more attractive than the often embarrassingly egotistical versions Smith had told before, as in the *Generall Historie*. Even the annoying habit of borrowing from his earlier writings to make new ones is restrained in the *Advertisements*. Smith borrowed only three paragraphs from his *Description of New England* and a few briefer passages from the *True Travels*. The former, also used in the *Generall Historie*, was well worth borrowing; for it is one of the brightest passages in Smith's writings. If Smith had written more prose as controlled as this, he would have a much larger claim to fame:

Seeing we are not born for ourselves but each to help other, and our abilities are much alike at the hour of our birth and minute of our death; seeing our good deeds or bad, by faith in Christ's merits, is all we have to carry our souls to heaven or hell; seeing honor is our lives' ambition, and our ambition after death to have an honorable memory of our life; and seeing by no means we would be abated of the dignity and glory of our predecessors, let us imitate their virtues to be worthily their successors, or at least not hinder, if not further, them that would do their utmost and best endeavor. (III, 277)

Because none of Smith's three New England publications has much structure or unity, and since each is uneven, most readers may be content with selections from the three, though the whole of the *Advertisements* is worth reading. Considerable advances in Smith's literary art are evident to one who reads the three in the order of composition (the first edition of *New Englands Trials* might be omitted): *A Description of New England* (1616), *New Englands Trials* (1622), and *Advertisements* (1631), for time and perspective permitted him to achieve wisdom and philosophic resignation without losing his excitedly optimistic vision of America, especially New England. Smith's final achievement, and his greatest as a writer, was the expression of his principles and practice in powerful language. In the last chapter of the *Advertisements*, his appreciation of the virtues that he believed he had demonstrated (when given the opportunity) is not obstructed by any petty-minded bitterness.

And truly there is no pleasure comparable to a generous spirit, as good employment in noble actions, especially amongst Turks, heathens, and infidels; to see daily new countries, people, fashions, governments, stratagems; relieve the oppressed, comfort his friends, pass miseries, subdue enemies, adventure upon any feasible danger for God and his country. It is true, it is a happy thing to be born to strength, wealth, and honor, but that which is got by prowess and magnanimity is the truest lustre, and those can the best distinguish content that have escaped most honorable dangers, as if, out of every extremity, he found himself now born to a new life, to learn how to amend and maintain his age. (III, 299)

The words are still stirring, especially when one remembers that Smith, a self-made man, achieved for himself a permanent place in history in a day when men could not easily rise from the station of their birth. If Smith had to exaggerate his own accomplishments to write prose such as this, the deception was well worthwhile.

Chapter Nine

Smith: An Assessment

The dominant concern of Captain John Smith's career as a writer was to obtain immediate results. He was eager to return to America; he wrote in order to persuade Englishmen to send him there. He hoped that his plans to combine fishing voyages and colonization would have immediate consequences. He described Virginia because published accounts were secondhand and inaccurate; he addressed his contemporaries, for whom he wanted to set the record straight. Why he published an autobiography is not clear, but he probably did so to make money. He wrote his two books of sea terms for the same reason. Even his big book, which was in theory "for the general good of all them who belong to those plantations [in America] and all their posterities" (II, 9), proves to be not only an argument that a tough Indian policy ought to be adopted immediately but also a defense of Smith against his detractors. Yet Smith's works have lived as have few nonbelletristic writings of his time. There is something of permanent interest about his subjects, his approaches, and the man himself. Perhaps an explanation can be found. It is worth trying, at any rate.

The Man Smith

First of all, there is the man. All of his efforts to impress backers with himself and his ideas, to serve as his own press agent, were unsuccessful in his own time; but because of them he lives on. His portrait published in *A Description of New England*, the account of his Virginia activities by his friends in *A Map of Virginia*, the editorializing that mars the *Generall Historie*, and the mature philosophizing of the *Advertisements*—all contribute to make Smith a recognizable human being in a way that few of his contemporaries are.

Smith told the story of his life mostly in bits and snatches, by digressions, by efforts to correct impressions and facts, by autobiography heavily interlaced with Virginia history or through New England propaganda. Only once, in *True Travels*, did he set out to tell his own story;

and then, ironically, he devoted much of his book to borrowed accounts of the lands he had visited. Nearly always Smith described his actions, not his feelings; and he set forth his thoughts only when he supposed that his ideas might lead to action.

One sees him as an active person, encountering Turks in single combat, killing the pasha of Nalbrits to escape captivity, exploring the northern edges of Chesapeake Bay, impressing Powhatan with his skills and his bravery, frightening the Indians into providing food for his men, mapping the New England coast, escaping from French pirates in a stormy night. He was tough, demanding, but always fair. Though frequently a leader of men, Smith seems to have been a loner. He liked independence: he left behind the ties of home and family, and he never married.

The image of himself that Smith created was largely a legitimate one, for research has shown that he either did or probably did all those improbable feats in distant lands he declared himself to have done. Specifically, he preserved the Virginia colony from collapse and gave a crucial impetus to interest in New England. But this self-reliant hero eventually painted a picture of himself that is decidedly overdrawn. It was a trifle pretentious of Smith to assert that he was "Admiral of New England" more than 15 years after his one visit there, even though, according to his statement, he had been given the title for life. It was preposterous for Smith to assert in 1626 that most of the American colonies sprang from the fruits of his adventures and discoveries, or to argue in 1629 that he had brought New England to the subjection of Great Britain. These statements are perhaps not lies, but they are surely exaggerations. To suppose, however, that such boasts demonstrate Smith's inability to appreciate the truth is not accurate. The fact seems to be that Smith could accept his frustration at being unable to return to America only by supposing that whatever was happening there was the consequence of his earlier, truly significant activities.

Smith was a practical man. He believed he should return to America because of his previous accomplishments and reputation there. He had specific proposals, carefully drawn up. He planned to make the Virginia and New England Indians work on behalf of the colonies, as the Spaniards had done; he wanted to establish colonies to work with the fishermen who visited the New England coast each year. Both plans were practical; and, if the former seems cruel, it was less so than the alternative adopted by the Virginia colonists, the elimination of the Indians by massacre. In his last work, the *Advertisements*, Smith threw out many practical suggestions for colonists and would-be colonists. And still he sought to return to America, even at 50, to put his ideas to work. The New Englanders will not succeed, wrote Smith in 1630, if they do not "in a short time cause the savages to do them as good service as their own men, as I did in Virginia, and yet neither use cruelty nor tyranny amongst them, a consequence well worth putting in practice, and till it be effected, they will hardly do well. I know ignorance will say it is impossible, but this impossible task, ever since the massacre in Virginia, I have been a suitor to have undertaken but with 150 men to have got corn, fortified the country, and discovered them more land than they all yet know or have demonstrated" (III, 293).

Smith was also a dreamer. He imagined a prosperous America, a place where a man could enjoy nature and its fruits. He urged cooperation in establishing colonies, but he saw no need for community. He was an individualist, and he wanted other men to have a chance to be as much. He urged men to imitate the "brave spirits that advanced themselves from poor soldiers to great captains, their posterity to great lords, and their king to be one of the greatest potentates on earth, and the fruits of their labors his greatest glory, power, and renown" (III, 301). He admired those men, such as Columbus, Cortez, Pizarro, and Magellan, who had shown themselves wise, discreet, generous, and courageous—his four favorite virtues.[1] He admired with Milton the desire for fame, "the spur that the clear spirit doth raise / (That last infirmity of noble mind) / To scorn delights, and live laborious days."

Above all, Smith was an American. One hundred and fifty years after Smith's death, St. Jean de Crèvecoeur was to ask, "What then is the American, this new man?" His answer might well have been Smith's: "The American," continued Crèvecoeur, "is a new man who acts upon new principles and must therefore entertain new ideas, and form new opinions. From involuntary idleness, servile dependence, penury, useless labor, he has passed to ample subsistence, to toils of a very different nature to what he had hitherto experienced. This is an American."[2] John Smith was such a new man. Smith is the most vivid personality of American literature before Benjamin Franklin.

John Smith is now recognized as the prototype of the American hero. John Seelye writes that "the American native hero who emerged from the wilderness context was to share a number of Captain Smith's traits: his courage, his cunning, his ingenuity, his faith in the future, his utilitarianism, and his generous way with the truth."[3] Alden T. Vaughan goes further when he writes that "in John Smith young America found a prototype of itself: bold, energetic, and optimistic; at the same time brash, intolerant, overly proud of its achievements, and overly solicitous of approval. Such a symbol fits with ease a boundless land, so laden with riches, and the aggressive settlers who conquered it."[4] The strongest statements of all come from J. A. Leo Lemay, whose recent book offers a whole catalogue of encomiums for Smith, among them these: "Captain John Smith fulfilled the heroic roles of both the European Renaissance and the American frontiersman." Smith was "the most courageous, industrious, persevering, skilled, benevolent, and humane person in early Virginia." "Captain John Smith was the greatest single founder of the English colonies in America."[5]

Smith the Writer

Captain John Smith was more than a vivid personality, a historic figure of unquestionable importance, and a propaganda writer who attracted attention to New England. He was also the author of works of permanent interest both for the picture they provide of America on the eve of colonization—the "Description" of Virginia and *A Description of New England*—and for the story that they tell of the Jamestown colonists' struggles—*A True Relation* and Book III of the *Generall Historie*.

Smith's most attractive works are the second and third books of the *Generall Historie*, the former, a "Description" of Virginia, polished into shape by an editor; the latter, Smith's revision and amplification of the work of other men. These two works, however composed, are masterful accounts of the place and the time: the land where England's first permanent American colony was established, and the first, crucial, two and a half years of the colony's life. In Smith's "Description," as Moses Coit Tyler has observed, "all the dull and hard details of the subject [are] made delightful by felicities of phrase that seem to spring up as easily as wild flowers in the woods of his own Virginia."[6] Smith's writings belong to American literature because he knew how to write and because he wrote about a subject of permanent interest to Americans.

The art of Book III has been largely ignored in the controversy over the Pocahontas story. Howard Mumford Jones called the earlier version, the *Proceedings*, an epic account.[7] The work of many writers with Smith's additions, Book III is significantly better. It is characterized by richness and literary integrity, and it is full of incident and character. Only recently has it been recognized for what it is by historians of literature. If Smith does not deserve all the credit for the final product, this fact should not continue to prevent the work itself from being recognized as a masterful narrative.

The treatment of Smith in the long-standard *Literary History of the United States* (1948) did a distinct disservice to an understanding of early American literature. The *Proceedings* is ignored in both its text and its bibliography, and concerning Book III of the *Generall Historie* again only the Pocahontas story receives attention: "Consider the Pocahontas story—and one cannot well avoid it. Smith's own account in 1608 is matter-of-fact. When he retold it in 1624, the story had been gorgeously and glamorously enlarged."[8] In fact, there is no "Pocahontas story" in the 1608 account; and the rescue by Pocahontas occupies less than a sentence in Smith's 1624 account (see Chapter 6).

True enough, Smith had a personal point to make in preparing Book III; yet it did not relate to Pocahontas. He used the *Generall Historie* to further his campaign to return to America. But critics might well be grateful to Smith for making available to a wide audience the best contemporary account of the beginning of the Virginia colony with valuable additions of his own. Smith was a writer only by force of circumstances, so he should be forgiven such subjectivity. If Smith's earlier account, *A True Relation*, is rather less good, it should be noted that it was written in great haste and was not intended for publication. Yet it has undeniable merits and is sometimes more detailed and graphic, as the following passages should demonstrate.

Proceedings (1612) and Book III (1624)

The next day Newport came ashore and received as much content as those people could give him: a boy named Thomas Savage was then given unto Powhatan, whom Newport called his son, for whom Powhatan gave him Namontack, his trusty servant and one of a shrewd, subtle capacity. (I, 216; II, 156)

A True Relation (1608)

But seeing Captain Newport and Master Scrivener coming ashore, the King returned to his house and I went to meet him [Newport]. With a trumpet before him, we marched to the King, who after his old manner kindly received him, especially a boy of thirteen years old, called Thomas Savage, whom he [Newport] gave him as his son. He requited this kindness with each of us a great basket of beans, and entertaining him with the former discourse, we passed away that day and agreed to bargain the next day, and so returned to our pinnace. (I, 69)

The fuller account of *A True Relation* is somewhat obscure, especially in its pronoun references; and it does not report the gift of Namontack, who was later important in the colonists' relations with the Indians. But the picture it provides is much more vivid.

The *Generall Historie* is difficult to evaluate as a whole. The fact that it is a large, unusually handsome book, not a thin pamphlet, has given it special importance. As a compilation, it has been long admired and read, especially by historically–minded Virginians, of whom there were and are many. But except for the second and third books and a portion of the sixth, it has no special authority; and, unlike Bradford's *Of Plymouth Plantation*, it is not susceptible to being trimmed and modernized for modern readers.

Any attempt to evaluate John Smith's writings leads inevitably to John Smith the man, just as any evaluation of the man requires an evaluation of his writings. As Richard Beale Davis notes of the *Generall Historie*, throughout "there is the sometimes haunting suggestion that this is a story of and by a man who realized he never quite achieved what he sought to achieve, a man of damaged ego."[9]

The best brief assessment yet written is that of Wayne Franklin in the *Columbia History of American Literature*. Franklin especially admires "the intensity of his vision of the New World as peculiarly his own domain, the space in which his identity is to be forged and defended. Here he represents the new contingency of American writing in general, its intimate engagement with geography. In him we may perceive for the first time that felt mixture of self and world, personality and place, which has made the role of space in American art as much an affair of the spirit as of topography pure and simple."[10] The world in which Smith describes himself as acting is not to be separated from the actor; the separation of the man from his works is thus an inappropriate separation, for the world of Captain John Smith's writings is truly Smith's own world, a world that emerges for him and for us as intimately associated with the describer.

A Description of New England, republished as a portion of Book VI of the *Generall Historie*, is also important among Smith's writings. Lacking the sense of form of Books II and III, it still has much to recommend it, especially a spirit of excitement about the discoveries that Smith had made and the plans they had inspired. Much better, however, is Smith's last pamphlet, *Advertisements For the unexperienced Planters of New England*. It too lacks an adequate organizing principle, but it is not so shapeless as the *Description of New England*. Its special virtue is the quality of its prose.

The prose of Smith's England is among the great glories of literature. In the *Advertisements* Smith gave America some of this inheritance.

His style, as in this passage from the preface, is perhaps best described as Elizabethan in its vigor and in its exuberant irregularity:

Apelles by the proportion of a foot could make the whole proportion of a man. Were he now living, he might go to school, for now are thousands can, by opinion, proportion kingdoms, cities, and lordships, that never durst adventure to see them. Malignancy I expect from those [that] have lived ten or twelve years in those actions and return as wise as they went, claiming time and experience for their tutor, that can neither shift [i.e., record the positions of] sun nor moon nor say their compass, yet will tell you of more than all the world, betwixt the Exchange, [St.] Paul's [Cathedral], and Westminster. So it be news, it matters not what that will pass current when truth must be stayed with an army of conceits that can make or mar anything, and tell as well what all England is by seeing but Milford Haven, as what Apelles was by the picture of his great toe. (III, 264)

The most admirable quality of Smith's style is concreteness. Smith's concern for fact and specific detail, his acute awareness of the world around him as he moved into unknown lands, gave him great assistance when he turned to writing. Time and again, sometimes unexpectedly, one finds in Smith's prose precise pictures of what he saw in the New World. Here, for example, is his description of the first churches in Virginia: "When I first went to Virginia [he wrote, 23 years later] I well remember we did hang an awning (which is an old sail) to three or four trees to shadow us from the sun. Our walls were rails of wood, our seats unhewed trees till we cut planks, our pulpit a bar of wood nailed to two neighboring trees. In foul weather we shifted into an old rotten tent, for we had few better. . . . This was our church, till we built a homely thing like a barn, set upon cratchets [poles], covered with rafts, sedge, and earth, so was also the walls" (III, 295). Smith's acute perceptiveness sometimes reveals itself in a sentence or a phrase, as in his observation on the trees of the New England coast: "Oak is the chief wood, of which there is great difference in regard of the soil where it groweth" (I, 342).

Just as Smith the man has been identified as the quintessential American hero, so have the themes of his writings been identified as "the very themes that would later become hallmarks of American literature": the Native Americans, America as wilderness, the importance of hard work, the recognition of individual merit over family status.[11] It is a special pleasure to read of Smith in the great work of the twentieth-century poet of Smith's Massachusetts coast, Charles Olson. In his

Maximus Poems he calls him affectionately "old mother Smith," quotes his poem "The Sea Mark," and expresses admiration for

> the eye he had
> for what New England offered,
> what we are other than theocratic, why we are
> not at all the Mediterraneans
> think we are.[12]

Captain John Smith is, then, for many reasons, a person of singular importance in the English colonization of America and a remarkable writer at the very beginning of American literature. Indeed, he was "an inspiring, thoughtful writer in treating such subjects as history, geography, the aspirations of life, and the vanity of existence."[13] On the pages of his writings one finds Smith almost palpably present. Readers who remember that bearded, forceful face may meet the person behind it as he tells us about the beginnings of what was to become the United States. Captain John Smith promised opportunities for the active, hardworking individual who would cross the waters to a world that Smith found wonderfully attractive, a world where abilities, not social standing, determined one's future. He did indeed have exaggerated notions about his own contributions, but recognizing this fact ought not prevent acknowledgment of his remarkable individual achievements and their importance in American development.

Notes and References

Preface

1. *The Complete Works of Captain John Smith (1580–1631)*, 3 vols. (published for the Institute of Early American History and Culture by the University of North Carolina Press, Chapel Hill and London, 1986). This edition is cited hereafter in the text.

2. Irene W. D. Hecht, review of *Works of Smith* by Philip L. Barbour, ed., *William and Mary Quarterly*, 3rd series, 44 (1987): 132.

3. There is, of course, American literature written in languages other than English, by Spanish writers such as Cabeza de Vaca (who describes a 1528 visit to Florida) or perhaps Frenchmen such as René Goulaine de Laudonnière, who wrote about the Florida of the 1560s—and there were prior Native American writers.

4. J. A. Leo Lemay, "Captain John Smith: American (?)," *Mississippi Studies in English*, 5 (1984–87): 288. Lemay subsequently set forth his ideas about Smith fully in *The American Dream of Captain John Smith* (Charlottesville and London: University Press of Virginia, 1991).

Chapter One

1. Irving Story, "Elizabethan Prelude," *Pacific University Studies in Literature*, No. 3 (November 1942): 11.

2. James A. Williamson, *The Age of Drake* (London: Adam and Charles Black, 1965), 52–129; S. T. Bindoff, *The Tudor Age* (New York: Penguin, 1964), 247–62.

3. James A. Williamson, *The Tudor Age* (New York: David McKay, 1964), 53–58, 70–71; Samuel Eliot Morison, *The European Discovery of America: The Northern Voyages A. D. 500–1600* (New York: Oxford University Press, 1971), 157–205. The extent of Cabot's voyage is now considered very uncertain.

4. Williamson, *Age of Drake*, 199, 231–34.

5. "A report of the voyage and successe thereof, attempted in the year of our Lord 1583 by sir Humfrey Gilbert knight," in Richard Hakluyt, *The Principal Navigations* (Glasgow: Hakluyt Society, 1903–1905), VIII, 60.

6. See George B. Parks, *Richard Hakluyt and the English Voyages* (New York: American Geographical Society, 1928); D. B. Quinn, ed., *The Hakluyt Handbook* (London: Hakluyt Society, 1974); and John Parker, *Books to Build an Empire* (Amsterdam: N. Israel, 1965).

7. The work is included in Eva G. R. Taylor, ed., *The Original Writings and Correspondence of the Two Richard Hakluyts* (London: Hakluyt Society, 1935).

8. David B. Quinn, *Raleigh and the British Empire* (London: Hodder and Stoughton, 1962), 58 ff.

9. A. L. Rowse, *The Expansion of Elizabethan England* (New York: St. Martin's Press, 1955), 209.

10. Louis B. Wright, *The Colonial Search for a Southern Eden* (University: University of Alabama Press, 1953), 7 ff.

11. Charles M. Andrews, *The Colonial Period in American History* (New Haven, Conn.: Yale University Press, 1933), 1: 20–21; Eva G. R. Taylor, *Late Tudor and Early Stuart Geography, 1583–1650* (London: Methuen, 1934), 2.

12. Taylor, *Geography*, 2–3.

13. James A. Williamson, *The Ocean in English History* (Westport, Conn.: Greenwood Press, 1979), 67.

14. Karen Kupperman, *Settling with the Indians: The Meeting of English and Indian Culture, 1580–1640* (Towana, N. J.: Rowman and Littlefield, 1980), 10. Needless to say, this motive was not identified in promotion propaganda.

15. Louis B. Wright, *Middle-Class Culture in Elizabethan England* (Ithaca, N.Y.: Cornell University Press, 1958), 508–35.

16. David B. Quinn, "Thomas Harriott and the New World," in *Thomas Harriott: Renaissance Scientist*, ed. John W. Shirley (Oxford: Clarendon Press, 1974), 36–43.

17. David B. Quinn, *The Roanoke Voyages, 1584–1590* (London: Hakluyt Society, 1955), 37. This is the best edition of Hariot's work. The best reproductions of White's drawings are in in *The American Drawings of John White*, two volumes, ed. David B. Quinn and Paul Hulton (London: Trustees of the British Museum; Chapel Hill: University of North Carolina Press, 1964). More accessible than this limited edition is *America 1585: The Complete Drawings of John White*, ed. Paul Hulton (London: British Museum Publications; Chapel Hill: University of North Carolina Press, 1984).

18. Thomas Harriott, *A brief and true report*, ed. Paul Hulton (New York: Dover, 1972), 16, 13, 22, 24. Subsequent references are to this text, a facsimile of the 1590 de Bry (English) edition.

19. Wayne Franklin, *Discoverers, Explorers, Settlers: The Diligent Writers of Early America* (Chicago: University of Chicago Press, 1979), 112.

20. A. L. Rowse, *The Elizabethans and America* (New York: Harper and Row, 1965), 189.

21. See Everett Emerson, "Thomas Hariot, John White, and Ould Virginia," in *Essays in Early Virginia Literature*, ed. J. A. Leo Lemay (New York: Burt Franklin, 1977).

22. It is to be found in Quinn, *Roanoke Voyages*, 255–94.

23. *The Discoverie of the large and bewtiful Empire of Guiana*, ed. V. T. Harlow (London: Argonaut, 1928), 1–li; this text is quoted hereafter.

24. Nicholas Monardes wrote *Joyfull Newest out of the Newfounde Worlde*, an account of American commodities, published in English in 1577.

25. C. S. Lewis, *English Literature in the Sixteenth Century* (Oxford: Oxford University Press, 1954), 437.

26. For information about Brereton and the voyage, see David B. Quinn and Alison M. Quinn, eds., *The English New England Voyages 1602–1608* (London: Hakluyt Society, 1983), and Warner F. Gookin and Philip L. Barbour, *Bartholomew Gosnold* (Hamden, Conn.: Archon Books, 1963). I use the text supplied by the Quinns. An account of this voyage by Gabriel Archer is in Samuel Purchas's *Purchas His Pilgrimes* and included in the Quinns' collection.

27. David B. Quinn, Alison M. Quinn, and Susan Hillier, *New American World* (New York: Arno Press and Hector Bye, 1979), III, 363.

28. David B. Quinn and Alison M. Quinn, *New England Voyages*, 248. I use the edition of Rosier that they provide. Supplemental remarks from the Rosier manuscript were published by Purchas in *Purchas His Pilgrimes* and are republished in the Quinns and Hillier, *New American World*, III, 381–91.

29. Ferdinando Gorges, *A briefe narration* (1658), as found in the Quinns, *New England Voyages*, 340.

30. Quinn and Quinn, *New England Voyages*, 86–90, 347–354.

31. I use the edition of Louis B. Wright entitled *A Voyage to Virginia in 1609* (Charlottesville: University Press of Virginia, 1964).

32. See Louis B. Wright and Virginia LaMar, eds., *The Tempest* (New York: Penguin, 1961), ix–xi, and Rowse, *The Elizabethans, and America*, 197–200.

33. Moses Coit Tyler, *A History of American Literature, 1607–1765* (New York: Putnam, 1878) 42–43.

34. See Alexander Whitaker, *Good Newes From Virginia* (London, 1613), with preface by William Crashaw; and Lewis Hughes, "A Letter Sent into England from the Summer Islands" (1615) in Louis B. Wright, *The Elizabethans' America* (Cambridge, Mass.: Harvard University Press, 1965), 202–05.

35. I use the edition of Louis B. Wright and Virginia Freund (London: Hakluyt Society, 1953).

36. Parks, *Richard Hakluyt*, 203–06, 219–22.

37. Taylor, *Geography*, 53.

38. Purchas, *Purchas His Pilgrimes* (London, 1619), sig. 41.

39. Parks, *Hakluyt*, 183–93, 223–25. Good accounts of Purchas are found in Loren E. Pennington, *Hakluytus Posthumus: Samuel Purchas and the Promotion of English Overseas Expansion* (Emporia State Research Studies, Kansas State College, 14, 1966); Philip L. Barbour, "Samuel Purchas: The Indefatigable Encyclopedist Who Lacked Good Judgment," in *Essays in Early Virginia Literature*, ed. J. A. Leo Lemay; and Louis B. Wright, *Religion and Empire* (Chapel Hill: University of North Carolina Press, 1943), 115–33.

40. For Coleridge's interest in Purchas, see John Livingston Lowes, *The Road to Xanadu* (Cambridge, Mass.: Harvard University Press, 1927).

41. Philip L. Barbour, *The Three World of Captain John Smith* (Boston: Houghton Mifflin, 1964), 354–55.

42. Louis B. Wright, *The Cultural Life of the American Colonies, 1607–1763* (New York: Harper and Row, 1962), 156.

Chapter Two

1. Bradford Smith, *Captain John Smith* (Philadelphia: Lippincott, 1953), 363.

2. B. Smith, *Smith*, 344.

3. Ian Beckwith, "Captain John Smith: The Yeoman Background," *History Today* 26 (1976): 450–51; B. Smith, *Smith*, 16–17.

4. See Mildred Campbell, *The English Yeoman under Elizabeth and the Early Stuarts* (New Haven, Conn.: Yale University Press, 1942).

5. B. Smith, *Smith*, 17–18.

6. Wallace Notestein, *The English People on the Eve of Colonization, 1603–1630* (New York: Harper and Row, 1962), 116–29.

7. Barbour, *Smith*, 11–16.

8. Barbour, *Smith*, 78 ff.

9. *Hakluytus Posthumus, or Purchas His Pilgrimes* (Glasgow: Hakluyt Society, 1905–1907), VII, 342.

10. The account of Smith's Virginia adventures is based on *The Proceedings of the English Colony in Virginia*, published in Smith, *Works*, and Barbour, *Smith*.

11. *The Jamestown Voyages Under the First Chapter 1606–1609*, ed. Philip L. Barbour (Cambridge, England: Hakluyt Society, 1969), I, 49, 51.

12. *Jamestown Voyages*, I, 78–79.

13. The account that follows is based on Smith's own accounts, chiefly in *A Description of New England* and *New Englands Trials*.

14. A full account is given by Barbour in *Pocahontas and Her World* (Boston: Houghton Mifflin, 1969), 155–59, 165–77.

Chapter Three

1. William Spengemann, *A Mirror for Americanists: Reflections on the Idea of American Literature* (Hanover, N.H.: University Press of New England, 1989), 9.

2. B. Smith, *Smith*, 116.

3. Barbour, *Smith*, 291–92.

4. Tyler, *American Literature*, I, 27.

5. Howard Mumford Jones, *The Literature of Virginia in the Seventeenth Century*, 2d ed. (Charlottesville: University Press of Virginia, 1968), 5, 121–22.

6. William C. Spengemann, "Early American Literature and the Project of Literary History," a paper—unpublished as of this writing—delivered at

Prospects: A Conference on Early American Literature in Chapel Hill, North Carolina, 1989, 29. Subsequent page references are in the text.

7. Ben McCary, *John Smith's Map of Virginia* (Williamsburg, Va.: Virginia 350th Anniversary-Celebration Corporation, 1957), 9.

8. Karen Kupperman notes that Smith's attitude toward "gentlemen" was ambiguous, for although he argued that what the colony needed was laborers, he also considered that gentlemen saved the colony—when they learned the necessary skills on the job. Karen Kupperman, *Settling with the Indians*, 148.

9. Glenn, "Captain John Smith and the Indians," *Virginia Magazine of History and Biography* 52 (1944): 228–48.

10. Pearce, *The Savages of North America*, rev. ed. (Baltimore: Johns Hopkins University Press, 1965), 14.

11. Kupperman, *Indians*, 107–40.

12. Lemay, *American Dream*, 119.

13. Miller, *Errand into the Wilderness* (New York: Harper and Row, 1964), 101–106.

14. Ben McCary, *Indians in Seventeenth-Century Virginia* (Williamsburg, Va.: Virginia 350th Anniversary–Celebration Corporation, 1957), 62–65. See also Regina Flannery, *An Analysis of Coastal Algonquian Culture* (Washington, D.C.: Catholic University of America Press, 1939), 94.

15. Philip L. Barbour, "The Riddle of the Powhatan Black Boyes," *Virginia Magazine of History and Biography* 88 (1980), 148–54.

16. Davis, *Intellectual Life in the Colonial South* (Knoxville: University of Tennessee Press, 1978), I, 22.

17. J. A. Leo Lemay appears to think that Smith wrote the speeches, but he also supposes that Smith took over accounts that others had written, "revised and expanded them, and made them into a connected story of early Virginia history" (Lemay, *American Dream*, 45). Like Barbour, I judge that the Rev. William Symonds played this role.

Chapter Four

1. Jarvis M. Morse, *American Beginnings* (Washington, D.C.: Public Affairs Press, 1952), 3.

2. Edwin C. Rozwenc, "Captain John Smith's Image of America," *William and Mary Quarterly*, 3rd series, 16 (1959), 28, 36.

3. Susan Myra Kingsbury, ed., *The Records of the Virginia Company of London* (Washington, D.C.: Government Printing Office, 1906–1935), I, 451–52.

4. Smith published his letter in the *Generall Historie*: *Complete Works*, II, 305–7.

5. Simpson, "The Act of Thought in Virginia," *Early American Literature* 14 (1979–80): 255.

6. Philip L. Barbour, "Captain John Smith and the Bishop of Sarum," *Huntington Library Quarterly* 26 (1962): 11–29.

7. Richard Hakluyt, *Principal Navigations*, VII, 297 ff.

8. Samuel Purchas, *Hakluytus Posthumus or Purchas His Pilgrimes*, 20 vols. (Glasgow: Hakluyt Society, extra series, 1903–1905).

9. In Purchas, *Pilgrimes*, XVIII, 335ff.

10. J. A. Leo Lemay mistakenly calls Book IV "the action-packed story of Smith's adventures in Virginia." Lemay, *American Dream*, 51. Presumably Lemay meant to refer to Book III.

11. See E. G. Swem and John M. Jennings, *A Selected Bibliography of Virginia, 1607–1699* (Williamsburg, Va.: 350th Anniversary Celebration Corporation, 1957).

12. J. Franklin Jameson, *The History of Historical Writing in America* (Boston: Houghton Mifflin, 1891), 6.

13. Not published until 1882, when J. H. Lefroy edited it (London: Hakluyt Society, 1882). Lefroy thought that Smith wrote the work because of the borrowings in the *Generall Historie*.

14. First published in *John Pory's Lost Description of Plymouth*, ed. Champlin Burrage (Boston: Houghton Mifflin, 1918). Smith referred to this work as "a plot of Richard Norwood" (II, 353). "A Plott or Mappe of Bermudas" was entered into the Stationers' Register on January 19, 1622, but no copy survives. Purchas published a version in *Pilgrimes*. See Barbour, *Works of Smith*, II, 338 (note).

15. See the edition of Henry Martyn Dexter (Boston: J. K. Wiggin, 1865), entitled *Mourt's Relation or Journal of the Plantation at Plymouth*, from which I quote.

16. Barbour in *Works of Smith*, III, 135.

17. Compare the statement in *Advertisements*, where Smith refers to those who, "having my books and maps, presumed they knew as much as they desired . . ." (III, 285).

18. Davis, *Intellectual Life*, I, 73.

19. Barbour, *Smith*, 368.

Chapter Five

1. Jarvis M. Morse, "Captain John Smith and His Critics," *Journal of Southern History* 1 (1935): 132.

2. Barbour, *Pocahontas*, 24.

3. At the end of this account, Smith notes, "Written by Anthony Bagnall, Nathanaell Powell, and Anas Todkill" (II, 180). The briefer account, in the *Proceedings*, is identified as being by Powell and Todkill. Barbour supposes that "Smith himself surely had a good deal to do with the end product"—*Works of Smith*, ed. Barbour, II, 180 (note).

4. Richard Beale Davis, *Literature and Society in Early Virginia* (Baton Rouge: Louisiana State University Press, 1973), 50.

5. Henry Adams, "Captain John Smith," *Chapters of Erie and Other Essays* (Boston: James R. Osgood, 1871). The original review in the *North American Review* 104 (1867): 1–30, does not include this statement.

6. Henry Adams, *The Letters of Henry Adams*, ed. J. C. Levenson and others (Cambridge, Mass.: Harvard University Press, 1982), I, 258–59. The whole statement of Adams's position in the letter is of interest.

7. Edward Wingfield's "Discourse" in Barbour, ed., *The Jamestown Voyages Under the First Charter, 1606–1609* (Cambridge, England: Hakluyt Society, 1969), I, 223.

8. Kevin J. Hayes, "Defining the Ideal Colonist: Captain John Smith's Revisions from *A True Relation* to the *Proceedings* to the *Generall Historie*," *Virginia Magazine of History and Biography* 99 (1991), 133.

Chapter Six

1. Barbour, *Works of Smith*, III, 6.

2. D. W. Waters, *The Art of Navigation in England in Elizabethan and Early Stuart Times* (New Haven, Conn.: Yale University Press, 1958), 467–68.

3. Philip L. Barbour, "Captain John Smith's Sea Grammar and Its Debt to Sir Henry Mainwaring's 'Seaman's Dictionary,'" *Mariner's Mirror* 58 (1972): 93–101, and Barbour, *Works of Smith*, III, 5–6, 42.

4. Waters, *Navigation*, passim.

5. Barbour notes that Smith erred twice: the borrowing is from Purchas's *Pilgrimes*, and Purchas himself was borrowing from Edward Brerewood's *Enquiries touching the Diversity of Languages, and Religions* (London, 1614). See *Works of Smith*, III, 95 (note).

6. See also Philip L. Barbour, "Two 'Unknown' Poems by Captain John Smith," *Virginia Magazine of History and Biography* 75 (1967): 157–58.

Chapter Seven

1. See Alden Vaughan, "John Smith Satirized: *The Legend of Captaine Iones*," *William and Mary Quarterly*, 3rd series, 45 (1988): 712–32.

2. Thomas Fuller, *The Historie of the Worthies of England* (London, 1662), 179–80.

3. See Charles Deane's edition of "A Discourse of Virginia" by Edward Maria Wingfield, in the American Antiquarian Society's *Archaelogica Americana*, 4 (1860): 67–103; Deane, ed., *A True Relation* (Boston: Wiggins and Lunt, 1866); Kropf, "Notes," *Notes and Queries*, 7th series, 9 (1890): 1–23, 41–43, 102–4, 161–62, 223–24, 281–82.

4. John Seelye, *Prophetic Waters: The River in Early American Life and Literature* (New York: Oxford University Press, 1977), 60.

5. Jones, *Literature of Virginia*, 54.

6. Jarvis M. Morse, "John Smith and His Critics: A Chapter in Colonial Historiography," *Journal of Southern History* 1 (1935): 130.

7. Barbour, *Smith*, 394.

8. Beckwith, "Yeoman," 450.

9. Barbour includes it in his edition as Fragment J, III, 341–63. Anyone interested in Smith's autobiography as an historical work should consult Barbour's notes to both the *True Travels* and the selection from Purchas.

10. All are identified in Barbour's edition.

11. Arber in *Travels and Works of Captain John Smith*, ed. Arber (Edinburgh: John Grant, 1910), I, xxv.

12. John Gould Fletcher, ed., *The True Travels* (New York: Rimington and Hooper, 1930), vi.

13. Barbour quotes George Lang's comment in his edition of *The Thoughts of the Emperor M. Aurelius Antoninus* (London: G. Bell, 1887): Smith "could not have found two writers better fitted to form the character of a soldier and a man" than *The Art of War* and the writings of Marcus Aurelius (26–27; quoted in *Works of Smith*, III, 156, note 10).

14. Paul Delany, *British Autobiography in the Seventeenth Century* (London: Routledge and Kegan Paul, 1969), 1, 116–17.

15. Philip F. Gura, "John *Who*?: Captain John Smith and Early American Literature," *Early American Literature* 21 (1986–87): 265. Of course Smith did not actually write in the "first person."

Chapter Eight

1. Samuel Eliot Morison, *Builders of the Bay Colony* (Boston: Houghton Mifflin, 1964), 6.

2. Henry F. Howe, *Prologue to New England* (New York: Farrar and Rinehart, 1943), 271.

3. Richard Arthur Preston, *Gorges of Plymouth Fort: A Life of Sir Ferdinando Gorges* (Toronto: University of Toronto Press, 1963), 159.

4. Barbour, *Smith*, 325, and Barbour, *Works of Smith*, I, 295.

5. Barbour's edition includes a leaf inserted in some copies that provides a list of the 30 names that Charles had changed (I, 319).

6. Stephen Innes, "Fulfilling John Smith's Vision," in *Work and Labor in Early America*, ed. Stephen Innes (Chapel Hill: University of North Carolina Press, 1988), 1–5, 9, 47.

7. Taylor, *Geography*, 167.

8. See Sigmund Diamond, "From Organization to Society: Virginia in the Seventeenth Century," *American Journal of Sociology* 63 (1958): 403–4.

9. George R. Stewart provides an account of Smith's contributions in his *Names on the Land* (Boston: Houghton Mifflin, 1958).

10. There is no documentary evidence that Smith was given this title, which he himself said was to be his during his life. See Smith, *Works*, I, 427, and 427 note 4.

11. Smith's letter seems to have resulted in Bacon's composition of his essay "Of Plantations," in which he echoes Smith's notions, such as his conviction that subsistence farming was fundamental to the success of a colony. See Lemay, *American Dream*, 48, and Taylor, *Geography*, 163.

12. Wilberforce Eames in *Bibliotheca Americana*, ed. Joseph Sabin and others (New York: Bibliographical Society of America, 1886–1937), XX, 248–49.

13. A. L. Rowse, *The Elizabethans and America*, 208.

14. A *sea mark* is an elevated object that serves to guide mariners.

15. Lemay, *American Dream*, 26.

16. The ecclesiastical polity of none of the churches founded by Winthrop's party was episcopal, and all abandoned the cross, the surplice, and the Prayer Book.

Chapter Nine

1. Smith has been effectively compared with the sixteenth-century Spanish explorer Bernal Diaz. See Nina M. Scott, "Bernal Diaz, Meet John Smith," *Americas* 33 (June–July 1981): 32–39.

2. From the holograph manuscript, Library of Congress, page 83. I am preparing a new edition of *Letters from an American Farmer*, with my wife, based on this holograph.

3. Seelye, *Prophetic Waters*, 80.

4. Alden J. Vaughan, *American Genesis: Captain John Smith and the Founding of Virginia* (Boston: Little, Brown, 1975), 190.

5. Lemay, *American Dream*, 4, 112, 226.

6. Tyler, *American Literature*, I, 31.

7. Jones, *Literature of Virginia*, 56.

8. R. G. Adams, "Reports and Chronicles," *Literary History of the United States*, ed. R. E. Spiller (New York: Macmillan, 1948), I, 33.

9. Davis, *Intellectual Life*, I, 69.

10. Wayne Franklin, in *Columbia Literary History of the United States* (New York: Columbia University Press, 1988), 21. Franklin's observation is very much like those of William Spengemann and Lewis Simpson, cited earlier in this study.

11. Alden T. Vaughan, "The Evolution of Virginia History: Early Historians of the First Colony," in *Perspectives on Early American History*, ed. Alden T. Vaughan and George A. Billias (New York: Harper and Row, 1973).

12. From "Some Good News," 130; "Maximus, to Gloucester," Letter 11,

54; and Letter 15, 73–74; *The Maximus Poems*, ed./trans. George Buttrick (Berkeley: University of California Press, 1983).

13. J. A. Leo Lemay, "Captain John Smith" in *The History of Southern Literature*, ed. Louis D. Rubin, Jr. (Baton Rouge: Louisiana State University Press, 1985), 33.

Selected Bibliography

PRIMARY SOURCES

Edited by Philip L. Barbour. *The Complete Works of Captain John Smith (1580–1631)*. 3 vols. Chapel Hill and London: Published for The Institute of Early American History and Culture by the University of North Carolina Press, 1986. A superb modern edition, complete with a biographical directory of such documents as Smith's will and epitaph (in St. Sepulchre's Church, London), a comprehensive bibliography (including a full listing of Barbour's many contributions to Smith studies) and more. See the acute review by J. A. Leo Lemay in *Southern Literary Journal* 20 (1987), 113–31. A one-volume selection of this edition is *Captain John Smith: A Select Edition of His Writings*, ed. Karen Ordahl Kupperman. Chapel Hill: University of North Carolina Press, 1988. It has a valuable introductory essay. Barbour had earlier written an excellent biography, *The Three Worlds of Captain John Smith* (1964).

Standard before Barbour's edition though incomplete was *Travels and Works of Captain John Smith*, edited by Edward Arber. A New Edition with a Biographical and Critical Introduction by A. G. Bradley. 2 vols. Edinburgh: John Grant, 1910. This edition was reprinted in 1966 by Burt Franklin, New York. Practically identical, except for Bradley's introduction and a sketchy bibliography by Thomas Seccombe, is Arber's edition in The English Scholar's Library, Birmingham, 1884, and Westminster, 1895.

Smith's works are listed below in chronological order. It has not seemed useful to cite publishers for works published before 1800. I list a few modern editions of importance.

A True Relation of such occurrences and accidents of noate as hath hapned in Virginia since the first planting of that Collony, which is now resident in the South part thereof, till the last returne from thence. London, 1608. In *Narratives of Early Virginia, 1606–1625*, edited by Lyon Gardiner Tyler. Original Narratives of Early American History. New York: Charles Scribner's Sons, 1907. And, with valuable notes, in *The Jamestown Voyages Under the First Charter 1606–1609*, edited by Philip L. Barbour. The Hakluyt Society. 2 vols. Cambridge: At the University Press, 1969.

"A Description of the Country, the Commodities, People, Government, and Religion," in *A Map of Virginia. With a Description of the Countrey, the Commodities, People, Government and Religion*. Oxford, 1612. Also in *Narratives of Early Virginia*, as above, and with useful introduction and notes, in Hakluyt Society edition of *The Jamestown Voyages*, as above.

The Proceedings of the English Colonie In Virginia since their first beginning from England in the yeare of our Lord 1606, till this present 1612, with all their accidents that befell them in their Journies and Discoveries. Also the Salvages discourses, orations and relations of the Bordering neighbours, and how they became subject to the English. Unfolding even the fundamentall causes from whence sprang so many miseries to the undertakers, and scandals to the businesse. . . . Oxford, 1612. Only portions are by Smith, probably chapters 1 and 2. Reproduced in the same collection as *A Map of Virginia* but with its own title page.

A Description of New England: Or the Observations, and discoveries, of Captain John Smith (Admirall of that Country) in the North of America, in the year of our Lord 1614; with the success of sixe Ships, that went the next yeare 1615; and the accidents befell him among the French men of warre: With the proofe of the present benefit this Countrey affoords; whither this present yeare, 1616, eight voluntary Ships are gone to make further tryall. London, 1616.

New Englands Trials. Declaring the successe of 26. Ships employed thither within these sixe yeares: with the benefit of that Countrey by sea and land; and how to build three score sayle of good ships, to make a little Navie Royall. London, 1620. Another publication, with a prefatory note by Charles Deane, Cambridge, Mass.: J. Wilson and Son, 1873.

New Englands Trials. Declaring the successe of 80 Ships employed thither within these eight yeares; and the benefit of that Countrey by Sea and Land. With the present estate of that happie Plantation, begun but by 60 weake men in the yeare 1620. And how to build a Fleete of good Shippes to make a little Navie Royall. 2d ed. London, 1622.

The generall History of Virginia, the Somer Isles, and New England, with the names of the Adventurers, and their adventures. [London, 1623.] An advance circular for the *Generall Historie.* Reprinted as *Captain John Smith's Circular or Prospectus of His Generall Historie of Virginia, New England, and the Summer Isles.* With notes by Luther S. Livingston. Cambridge: Privately printed, 1924.

The Generall Historie of Virginia, New-England, and the Summer Isles: with the names of the Adventurers, Planters, and Governours from their first beginning An°: 1584, to this present 1624. With the Proceedings of those Severall Colonies and the Accidents that befell them in all their Journyes and Discoveries. Also the Maps and Descriptions of all those Countryes, their Commodities, people, Government, Customes, and Religion yet knowne. Divided into sixe Bookes. London, 1624. Reissued in 1625, 1626, 1627, 1631, and 1632. Facsimile reprint: Cleveland: World Publishing Company, 1966. Historical introduction by A. L. Rowse; bibliographical notes by Robert O. Dougan. Another facsimile: Ann Arbor: University Microfilms, 1967. Extracts appear in *Captain John Smith's History of Virginia: A Selection,* edited by David Freeman Hawke. Indianapolis and New York: Bobbs-Merrill, 1970.

"To The Worshipfull the Master Wardens & Societie of the Cordwayners of ye Cittie of London." A letter in the Huntington Library copy of the *Generall Historie,* published in Smith bibliography, *Bibliotheca Americana,* edited by

Joseph Sabin and others. New York: Bibliographical Society of America, 1869–1937. 29 vols. XX, 238. Also in Louis B. Wright, ed. *The Elizabethans' America*. Cambridge, Mass.: Harvard University Press, 1965.

An Accidence Or The Path-way to Experience. Necessary for all Young Sea-men, or those that are desirous to goe to Sea, briefly shewing the Phrases, Offices, and Words of Command, Belonging to the Building, Ridging, and Sayling, a Man of Warre: And how to manage at Fight at Sea. Together with the Charge and Duty of every Officer, and their Shares: Also the Names, Weight, Charge, Shot, and Powder, of all sorts of great Ordnance. With the use of the Petty Tally. London, 1626.

A Sea Grammar, With The Plaine Exposition of Smiths Accidence for young Sea-men, enlarged. Divided into fifteene Chapters: what they are you may partly conceive by the Contents. London, 1627. Subsequent editions 1653, 1691, 1692, 1699, entitled *The Sea-mans Grammar.* Also edited by Kermit Goell. London: Michael Joseph, 1970.

"John Smith of his friend Master John Taylor and his Armado." In John Taylor, *An Armado.* London, 1627. Also in "Two 'Unknown' Poems by Captain John Smith." Edited by Philip L. Barbour. *Virginia Magazine of History and Biography* 75 (1967), 157–58.

"In the due Honor of the Author Master Robert Norton, and his Worke." *The Gunner.* Edited by Robert Norton. London, 1628. Also in "Two 'Unknown' Poems," as above.

The True Travels, Adventures, and Observations of Captaine John Smith, In Europe, Asia, Affrica, and America, from Anno Domini 1593 to 1629. His Accidents and Sea-fights in the Straights; his Service and Stratagems of warre in Hungaria, Transilvania, Wallachia, and Moldavia, against the Turkes, and Tartars; his three single combats betwixt the Christian Armie and the Turkes. After how he was taken prisoner by the Turks, sold for a Slave, sent into Tartaria; his description of the Tartars, their strange manners and customes of Religions, Diets, Buildings, Warres, Feasts, Ceremonies, and Living; how hee slew the Bashaw of Nalbrits in Cambia, and escaped from the Turkes and Tartars. Together with a continuation of his generall History of Virginia, Summer-Iles, New England, and their proceedings, since 1624, to this present 1629; as also of the new Plantations of the great River of the Amazons, the Iles of St. Christopher, Mevis, and Barbados in the West Indies. All written by actuall Authuors, whose names you shall finde along the History. London, 1630. Published also as *The True Travels and Adventures of Captain John Smith,* edited by Alexander J. Philip. London and New York: Routledge, 1907. With an introduction by John Gould Fletcher and bibliographical note by Lawrence C. Wroth. New York: Rimington & Hooper, 1930.

Advertisements For the unexperienced Planters of New England, or any where. Or, The Path-way to experience to erect a Plantation. With the yearely proceedings of this Country in Fishing and planting, since the yeare 1614. To the yeare 1630. And their present estate. Also how to prevent the greatest inconveniences, by their proceedings in Virginia, and other Plantations, by approved examples. With the Countries Armes, a description of the Coast, Harbours, Habitations, Land-markes. Latitude and Longitude: with the Map, allowed by our Royall King Charles. London, 1631. Somewhat abridged in *Captain John Smith's America: Selections From His Writings,* edited by John Lankford, New York: Harper & Row, 1967.

SECONDARY SOURCES

Bibliographies

Eames, Wilberforce. "Bibliography of Captain John Smith." In *Bibliotheca Americana: A Dictionary of Books Relating to America,* edited by Joseph Sabin, et al. 29 vols. New York: Bibliographical Society of America, 1868–1937. XX, 218–63. Reprinted separately. New York: Bibliographical Society of America, 1927. Extremely valuable.

Quinn, David B. "Bibliography." In *The Complete Works of Captain John Smith (1580–1631).* 3 vols. Chapel Hill: University of North Carolina Press, 1986. III, 393–433. This bibliography lists all the works cited in the Barbour edition.

Hayes, Kevin J. *Captain John Smith: A Reference Guide.* Boston: G. K. Hall, 1991. An excellent secondary bibliography, especially useful for consideration of Smith's reputation.

Books and Parts of Books

Barbour, Philip L. *Pocahontas and Her World.* Boston: Houghton Mifflin, 1970. A useful discussion of Pocahontas's relationship to Smith, the Virginia Indians, and related matters.

————. *The Three Worlds of Captain John Smith.* Boston: Houghton Mifflin, 1964. Authoritative biography.

Davis, Richard Beale. *Intellectual Life in the Colonial South, 1585–1763.* 3 vols. Knoxville: University of Tennessee Press, 1978. Magisterial overview, with Smith a major figure.

Gummere, Richard M. *The American Colonial Mind and the Classical Tradition.* Cambridge, Mass.: Harvard University Press, 1963. Includes a half-dozen pages on Smith's classical interests but reaches no profound conclusions.

Hubbell, Jay B. "The Smith–Pocahontas Literary Legend." In *South and Southwest, Literary Essays and Reminiscences,* edited by Jay B. Hubbell. Durham, N.C.: Duke University Press, 1965. The best account of the uses to which Smith's story has been put.

Innes, Stephen. "Fulfilling John Smith's Vision: Work and Labor in Early America." In *Work and Labor in Early America,* edited by Stephen Innes. Chapel Hill: University of North Carolina Press, 1988. Describes Smith's vision and how it was implemented.

Jameson, J. Franklin. *The History of Historical Writings in America*. Boston: Houghton Mifflin, 1891. Still useful for its evaluation of Smith's writings.

Jones, Howard Mumford. *The Literature of Virginia in the Seventeenth Century*. In *Memoirs*, The American Academy of Arts and Sciences, XIX (1914–46). Part 2. Boston, 1946. 2d edition, Charlottesville: University Press of Virginia, 1968. Twenty pages are devoted to Smith. Somewhat impressionistic, but useful because of the context.

Lankford, John, ed. *Captain John Smith's America: Selections From His Writings*. New York: Harper & Row, 1967. Includes a 21-page essay on Smith. One of the best accounts of Smith as historian.

Lemay, J. A. Leo. *The American Dream of Captain John Smith*. Charlottesville: University Press of Virginia, 1991. A generous, even at times extravagantly admiring account, with chapters on Smith as promoter and as travel writer, Smith and the Indians, and Smith's role in the creation of American ideals, among others. A full, if not overful appreciation of Smith's contributions to American colonization and American culture.

———. "Captain John Smith." In *The History of Southern Literature*, edited by Louis D. Rubin. Baton Rouge: Louisiana State University Press, 1985. An intelligent and admiring appraisal.

Morison, Samuel Eliot. *Builders of the Bay Colony*. Boston: Houghton Mifflin, 1964. See chapter 1, "Promoters and Precursors: Richard Hakluyt, Captain John Smith, and Morton of Merrymount"; not wholly fair in its remarks on Smith's veracity but useful nonetheless.

Morse, Jarvis M. *American Beginnings*. Washington, D.C.: Public Affairs Press, 1952. Comments knowledgeably on Smith as historian.

Morton, Richard L. *Colonial Virginia*. 2 vols. Chapel Hill: University of North Carolina Press, 1960. Full history of the colony. Morton praises Smith's work as leader of Jamestown.

Rowse, A. L. *The Elizabethans and America*. New York: Harper and Brothers, 1965. Important background study, with passing references to Smith.

Seelye, John. *Prophetic Waters: The River in Early American Life and Literature*. New York: Oxford University Press, 1977. Contains a lively and entertaining chapter, "Captain Courageous: Captain Smith, Father of Us All."

Smith, Bradford. *Captain John Smith: His Life & Legend*. Philadelphia: J. B. Lippincott, 1953. Though superseded by Barbour's biography, still worth consulting. Includes as an appendix, "Captain John Smith's Hungary and Transylvania," by Laura Polanyi Striker.

Taylor, Eva G. R. *Late Tudor and Early Stuart Geography, 1583–1650*. London: Methuen & Co., 1934. Considers Smith in the context of geographical literature.

Tyler, Moses Coit. *A History of American Literature, 1607–1765*. New York: G. P. Putnam's Sons, 1878; New York: Collier Books, 1962. Still the standard history; a whole chapter is devoted to Smith.

Vaughan, Alden T. *American Genesis: Captain John Smith and the Founding of Virginia.* Boston: Little, Brown, 1975. Library of American Biography. A learned account of Smith in the context of the early history of Virginia.

Articles

Beckwith, Ian. "Captain John Smith: The Yeoman Background." *History Today* 26 (1976): 444–51. Provides information about Smith's prosperous family.

Morse, Jarvis M. "Captain John Smith and His Critics: A Chapter in Colonial Historiography." *Journal of Southern History* 1 (1935): 123–37. Very valuable survey of Smith's writings and commentators on them.

Rozwenc, Edwin C. "Captain John Smith's Image of America." *William and Mary Quarterly*, 3rd series, 16 (1959): 27–36. Perceptive study. Argues that Smith gave the English a "vision of America as a place in which to achieve personal honor and glory."

Scott, Nina M. "Bernal Diaz, Meet John Smith." *Americas* 33 (1981): 32–39. Finds analogies between Smith and the sixteenth-century Spanish explorer.

Simpson, Lewis P. "The Act of Thought in Virginia." *Early American Literature* 14 (1979–80): 253–68. Shows how Smith made the *Generall Historie* a union of self, letters, and secular history.

Striker, Laura P. and Bradford Smith. "The Rehabilitation of Captain John Smith." *Journal of Southern History* 28 (1962): 474–81. Best treatment of the subject, but written before most of Barbour's studies.

Vaughan, Alden T. "John Smith Satirized: *The Legend of Captaine Iones.*" *William and Mary Quarterly*, third series, 45 (1988): 712–32. Shows that David Lloyd satirized Smith in a 1631 poem and that doubts about Smith's veracity were widely held in his own time.

Background Information

Andrews, Charles M. *The Colonial Period of American History.* 4 vols. New Haven, Conn.: Yale University Press, 1934. First volume provides a very helpful overview of America's colonization.

Barbour, Philip L. "Samuel Purchas: The Indefatigable Enclyclopedist Who Lacked Good Judgment." In *Essays in Early Virginia Literature*, edited by J. A. Leo Lemay. New York: Burt Franklin, 1977. Shows Purchas's indebtedness to Smith.

Craven, Wesley Frank. *The Southern Colonies in the Seventeenth-Century, 1607–1689.* Baton Rouge: Louisiana State University Press, 1949. A comprehensive study.

Cumming, W. P., R. A. Skelton, and D. B. Quinn. *The Discovery of North*

America. New York: American Heritage Press, 1972. A handsome collection of documents and maps, plus illustrations.

Jones, Howard Mumford. "The Colonial Impulse: An Analysis of the 'Promotion' Literature of Colonization." *Proceedings of the American Philosophical Society*, 90 (1946): 131–61. Because much of what Smith wrote was promotion literature, a relevant and useful study.

————. *O Strange New World. American Culture: The Formative Years.* New York: The Viking Press, 1964. Very important background study, discursive and suggestive.

Morison, Samuel Eliot. *The European Discovery of America: The Northern Voyages, A. D. 500–1600.* New York: Oxford University Press, 1971. A big, thorough, readable account.

Notestein, Wallace. *The English People on the Eve of Colonization, 1603–1630.* New York: Harper and Brothers, 1954. Chapters on Smith's England, leading to one on "The Companies and Colonization."

Parker, John. *Books to Build an Empire. A Bibliographical History of English Overseas Interests to 1620.* Amsterdam: N. Israel, 1965. A solid and scholarly treatment of the topic to which the title clearly points.

Pennington, Loren E. *Hakluytus Posthumus: Samuel Purchas and the Promotion of Overseas Expansion.* Emporia, Kansas: Emporia State Research Studies, 14 (1966). A 34-page pamphlet.

Penrose, Boies. *Travel and Discovery in the Renaissance, 1420–1620.* Cambridge: Harvard University Press, 1952. Lively general study.

Quinn, David B. *England and the Discovery of America, 1481–1620.* New York: Knopf, 1974. A valuable collection of essays.

————. *Raleigh and the British Empire.* London: The English Universities Press, 1962. Smith's and Raleigh's interests overlapped.

————, ed. *The Roanoke Voyages, 1584–1590.* 2 vols. London: Hakluyt Society, 1955. Collection of documents, skillfully edited, including Hariot's book.

————, Alison M. Quinn, and Susan Hillier, eds. *New American World: A Documentary History of North America to 1612.* 5 vols. New York: Arno Press and Hector Bye, 1979. See especially volume 3, *English Plans for North America. The Roanoke Voyages, New England Ventures.*

Rowse, A. L. *The Expansion of Elizabethan England.* New York: St. Martin's Press, 1955. Includes valuable and fresh chapter on American colonization.

Steele, Colin R. "From Hakluyt to Purchas." In *The Hakluyt Handbook*, edited by David B. Quinn. 2 vols. London: Hakluyt Society, 1974. A useful description of the relationship.

Story, Irving C. "The Elizabethan Prelude." *Pacific University Studies in Literature*, No. 3, November 1942. Relates Smith to Hakluyt.

Williamson, James A. *The Tudor Age.* 3rd edition. New York: David McKay Company, 1964. Emphasizes exploration and colonization.

Wright, Louis B. *The Colonial Search for a Southern Eden*. University: University
of Alabama Press, 1953. A brief but thoughtful study.

———, ed. *The Elizabethans' America: A Collection of Early Reports by Englishmen
on the New World*. Cambridge, Mass.: Harvard University Press, 1965.
Includes four selections from Smith among its 42 pieces.

———. *Middle-Class Culture in Elizabethan England*. Ithaca, N.Y.: Cornell
University Press, 1958. On the vogue of travel literature.

———. *Religion and Empire: The Alliance between Piety and Commerce in English
Expansion, 1558-1625*. Chapel Hill: University of North Carolina Press,
1943.

Index

The Author

Everett Emerson, Alumni Distinguished Professor of English and American Studies at the University of North Carolina, is a noted specialist on early American literature. For 20 years he edited the journal *Early American Literature*. His other books include *John Cotton; English Puritanism from John Hooper to John Milton; Major Writers of Early American Literature; American Literature 1764–1789: The Revolutionary Years; Puritanism in America, 1620–1750*; and *Letters from New England, 1629–1638*. In 1990 he was recognized by the Modern Language Association as Honored Scholar of Early American Literature. Professor Emerson is the author of *The Authentic Mark Twain: A Literary Biography of Samuel L. Clemens* and founder of the Mark Twain Circle of America, which has recognized him as an honored life member. He is an honorary member of the Emily Dickinson Society of Japan, the American Studies Association of Thailand, and the American Society for 18th Century Studies, and has lectured widely in this country and abroad.